PENGUIN BOOKS — GREAT IDEAS

Fear and Trembling

Søren Kierkegaard

1813–1855

Søren Kierkegaard

Fear and Trembling

TRANSLATED BY
ALASTAIR HANNAY

PENGUIN BOOKS — GREAT IDEAS

PENGUIN BOOKS

Published by the Penguin Group
Penguin Group (USA) Inc., 375 Hudson Street, New York, New York 10014, U.S.A.
Penguin Group (Canada), 90 Eglinton Avenue East, Suite 700, Toronto,
Ontario, Canada M4P 2Y3 (a division of Pearson Penguin Canada Inc.)
Penguin Books Ltd, 80 Strand, London WC2R 0RL, England
Penguin Ireland, 25 St Stephen's Green, Dublin 2, Ireland (a division of Penguin Books Ltd)
Penguin Group (Australia), 250 Camberwell Road, Camberwell,
Victoria 3124, Australia (a division of Pearson Australia Group Pty Ltd)
Penguin Books India Pvt Ltd, 11 Community Centre, Panchsheel Park, New Delhi – 110 017, India
Penguin Group (NZ), cnr Airborne and Rosedale Roads, Albany,
Auckland 1310, New Zealand (a division of Pearson New Zealand Ltd)
Penguin Books (South Africa) (Pty) Ltd, 24 Sturdee Avenue,
Rosebank, Johannesburg 2196, South Africa

Penguin Books Ltd, Registered Offices:
80 Strand, London WC2R 0RL, England

This edition published in Penguin Books (UK) 2005
Published in Penguin Books (USA) 2006

3   5   7   9   10   8   6   4   2

Translation copyright © Alastair Hannay, 1985
All rights reserved

Reprinted from *Fear and Trembling*,
translated and introduced by Alastair Hannay (Penguin Classics, 1985).

ISBN 0 14 30.3757 9
CIP data available

Printed in the United States of America
Set in Monotype Dante

Except in the United States of America, this book is sold subject to the condition
that it shall not, by way of trade or otherwise, be lent, resold, hired out, or otherwise
circulated without the publisher's prior consent in any form of binding or cover other
than that in which it is published and without a similar condition including
this condition being imposed on the subsequent purchaser.

The scanning, uploading and distribution of this book via the Internet or via any
other means without the permission of the publisher is illegal and punishable by law.
Please purchase only authorized electronic editions, and do not participate in or encourage
electronic piracy of copyrighted materials. Your support of the author's rights is appreciated.

Contents

Fear and Trembling

What Tarquin the Proud said in his garden with the poppy blooms was understood by the son but not by the messenger.

HAMANN

Preface

Not just in commerce but in the world of ideas too our age is putting on a veritable clearance sale. Everything can be had so dirt cheap that one begins to wonder whether in the end anyone will want to make a bid. Every speculative score-keeper who conscientiously marks up the momentous march of modern philosophy, every lecturer, crammer, student, everyone on the outskirts of philosophy or at its centre is unwilling to stop with doubting everything. They all go further. It would perhaps be malapropos to inquire where they think they are going, though surely we may in all politeness and respect take it for granted that they have indeed doubted everything, otherwise it would be odd to talk of going further. This preliminary step is one they have all of them taken, and presumably with so little effort as to feel no need to drop some word about how; for not even someone genuinely anxious for a little enlightenment on this will find such. Not a gesture that might point him in the right direction, no small dietary prescription for how to go about such a huge task. 'But Descartes did it, didn't he?' A venerable, humble, honest thinker whose writings surely no one can read without being most deeply stirred – Descartes must have done what he has said and said what he has done. A rare enough occurrence in our own time! Descartes, as he himself repeatedly insists, was no doubter in matters of faith. ('[B]ut we must keep in mind what has been said, that we must trust to this natural light only so long as nothing contrary to it is revealed by God himself . . . Above all we should impress on our memory as an infallible rule that what God has revealed to us is incomparably more certain than anything else; and that we ought to submit to the Divine authority rather than to our own judgement even though the light of reason may seem to us to suggest, with the utmost clearness and evidence, something opposite' [from Principles 28 and 76 of *Principles of Philosophy*].) Descartes has not cried 'Fire!' and made it everyone's duty to doubt, for Descartes was a quiet and lonely thinker, not a bellowing streetwatch; he was modest enough to allow that his method was important only for himself and sprang partly from his own earlier bungling with knowledge. ('Thus my design here is not to teach the Method which everyone should follow in order to promote the good conduct of Reason, but only to show in what manner I have endeavoured to conduct my own . . . But so soon as I had achieved the entire course of study [that is, of his youth – Johannes *de silentio*'s interpolation] at the close of which one is usually received into the ranks of the learned, I entirely changed my opinion. For I found myself embarrassed with so many doubts and errors that it seemed to me that the effort to instruct myself had no effect other than the increasing discovery of my own ignorance' [*Discourse on the Method of Rightly Conducting the Reason and Seeking the Truth in the Sciences*].) – What those old Greeks, whom one must also credit with a little knowledge of philosophy, took to be the task of a whole lifetime, doubt not being a skill one acquires in days and weeks; what the old veteran warrior achieved after keeping the balance of doubt in the face of all inveiglements, fearlessly rejecting the certainties of sense and thought, incorruptibly defying selfish anxieties and the wheedling of sympathies – that is where nowadays everyone begins.

Today nobody will stop with faith; they all go further. It would perhaps be rash to inquire where to, but surely a mark of urbanity and good breeding on my part to assume that in fact everyone does indeed have faith, otherwise it would be odd to talk of going further. In those old days it was different. For then faith was a task for a whole lifetime, not a skill thought to be acquired in either days or weeks. When the old campaigner approached the end, had fought the good fight, and kept his faith, his heart was still young enough not to have forgotten the fear and trembling that disciplined his youth and which, although the grown man mastered it, no man altogether outgrows – unless he somehow manages at the earliest possible opportunity to go further. Where these venerable figures arrived our own age begins, in order to go further.

The present author is no philosopher, he has not understood the System, nor does he know if there really is one, or if it has been completed. As far as his own weak head is concerned the thought of what huge heads everyone must have in order to have such huge thoughts is already enough. Even if one were able to render the whole of the content of faith into conceptual form, it would not follow that one had grasped faith, grasped how one came to it, or how it came to one. The present author is no philosopher, he is *poetice et eleganter* [to put it in poetic and well-chosen terms], an occasional copyist who neither writes the System nor makes any *promises* about it, who pledges neither anything about the System nor himself *to* it. He writes because for him doing so is a luxury, the more agreeable and conspicuous the fewer who buy and read what he writes. In an age where passion has been done away with for the sake of science he easily foresees his fate – in an age when an author who wants readers must be careful to write in a way that he can be comfortably leafed through during the after-dinner nap, and be sure to present himself to the world like the polite gardener's boy in the *Advertiser* who, hat in hand and with good references from his previous place of employment, recommends himself to a much-esteemed public. He foresees his fate will be to be completely ignored; has a dreadful foreboding that the scourge of zealous criticism will more than once make itself felt; and shudders at what terrifies him even more, that some enterprising recorder, a paragraph swallower who to rescue learning is always willing to do to others' writings what, to 'preserve good taste', Trop nobly did to *The Destruction of the Human Race*, will slice him into sections as ruthlessly as the man who, in the service of the science of punctuation, divided up his speech by counting the words and putting a full-stop after every fifty and a semi-colon after every thirty-five. No, I prostrate myself before any systematic bag-searcher; this is not the System, it hasn't the slightest thing to do with the System. I wish all good on the

System and on the Danish shareholders in that omnibus; for it will hardly become a tower. I wish them good luck and prosperity one and all.

Respectfully
Johannes *de silentio*

Attunement

There was once a man; he had learned as a child that beautiful tale of how God tried Abraham, how he withstood the test, kept his faith and for the second time received a son against every expectation. When he became older he read the same story with even greater admiration, for life had divided what had been united in the child's pious simplicity. The older he became the more often his thoughts turned to that tale, his enthusiasm became stronger and stronger, and yet less and less could he understand it. Finally it put everything else out of his mind; his soul had but one wish, actually to see Abraham, and one longing, to have been witness to those events. It was not the beautiful regions of the East, nor the earthly splendour of the Promised Land, he longed to see, not the God-fearing couple whose old age God had blessed, not the venerable figure of the patriarch stricken in years, not the youthful vigour God gave to Isaac – it would have been the same if it had taken place on a barren heath. What he yearned for was to accompany them on the three-day journey, when Abraham rode with grief before him and Isaac by his side. He wanted to be there at that moment when Abraham raised his eyes and saw in the distance the mountain in Moriah, the moment he left the asses behind and went on up the mountain alone with Isaac. For

8

what occupied him was not the finely wrought fabric of imagination, but the shudder of thought.

This man was no thinker, he felt no need to go further than faith. To be remembered as its father seemed to him to be surely the greatest glory of all, and to have it a lot to be envied even if no one else knew.

This man was no learned exegete, he knew no Hebrew; had he known Hebrew then perhaps it might have been easy for him to understand the story of Abraham.

I

And it came to pass after these things, that God did tempt Abraham, and said unto him . . . Take now thy son, thine only son Isaac, whom thou lovest, and get thee into the land of Moriah; and offer him there for a burnt offering upon one of the mountains which I will tell thee of.

It was early morning. Abraham rose in good time, had the asses saddled and left his tent, taking Isaac with him, but Sarah watched them from the window as they went down the valley until she could see them no more. They rode in silence for three days; on the morning of the fourth Abraham still said not a word, but raised his eyes and saw afar the mountain in Moriah. He left the servants behind and went on alone up the mountain with Isaac beside him. But Abraham said to himself: 'I won't conceal from Isaac where this way is leading him.' He stood still, laid his hand on Isaac's head to give him his blessing, and Isaac bent down to receive it. And Abraham's expression was fatherly, his gaze gentle, his speech encouraging. But Isaac could not understand him, his soul could not be uplifted; he clung to Abraham's knees, pleaded at his feet, begged for his young life, for his fair promise; he called to mind the joy in Abraham's house, reminded him of the sorrow and loneliness. Then Abraham lifted the boy up and walked with him, taking him by the hand, and his words were full of comfort and exhortation. But Isaac could not understand him. Abraham climbed the mountain in Moriah, but Isaac did not understand him. Then he turned away from Isaac for a moment, but when Isaac saw his face a second time it was changed, his gaze was wild, his mien one of horror. He caught Isaac by the chest, threw him to the ground and said: 'Foolish boy, do you believe I am your father? I am an idolater. Do you believe this is God's command? No, it is my own desire.' Then Isaac trembled and in his anguish cried: 'God in heaven have mercy on me, God of Abraham have mercy on me; if I have no father on earth, then be Thou my father!' But below his breath Abraham said to himself: 'Lord in heaven I thank Thee; it is after all better that he believe I am a monster than that he lose faith in Thee.'

*

When the child is to be weaned the mother blackens her breast, for it would be a shame were the breast to look pleasing when the child is not to have it. So the child believes that the breast has changed but the mother is the same, her look loving and tender as ever. Lucky the one that needed no more terrible means to wean the child!

II

It was early morning. Abraham rose in good time, embraced Sarah, the bride of his old age, and Sarah kissed Isaac, who had taken her disgrace from her, was her pride and hope for all generations. So they rode on in silence and Abraham's eyes were fixed on the ground, until the fourth day when he looked up and saw afar the mountain in Moriah, but he turned his gaze once again to the ground. Silently he arranged the fire-wood, bound Isaac; silently he drew the knife. Then he saw the ram that God had appointed. He sacrificed that and returned home . . . From that day on, Abraham became old, he could not forget that God had demanded this of him. Isaac throve as before; but Abraham's eye was darkened, he saw joy no more.

*

When the child has grown and is to be weaned the mother virginally covers her breast, so the child no more has a mother. Lucky the child that lost its mother in no other way!

III

It was early morning. Abraham rose in good time, kissed Sarah the young mother, and Sarah kissed Isaac, her delight, her joy for ever. And Abraham rode thoughtfully on. He thought of Hagar and of the son whom he had driven out into the desert. He climbed the mountain in Moriah, he drew the knife.

It was a tranquil evening when Abraham rode out alone, and he rode to the mountain in Moriah: he threw himself on his face, he begged God to forgive him sin at having been willing to sacrifice Isaac, at the father's having forgotten his duty to his son. He rode more frequently on his lonely way, but found no peace. He could not comprehend that it was a sin to have been willing to sacrifice to God the best he owned; that for which he would many a time have gladly laid down his own life; and if it was a sin, if he had not so loved Isaac, then he could not understand that it could be forgiven; for what sin was more terrible?

⋆

When the child is to be weaned the mother too is not without sorrow, that she and the child grow more and more apart; that the child which first lay beneath her heart, yet later rested at her breast, should no longer be so close. Thus together they suffer this brief sorrow. Lucky the one who kept the child so close and had no need to sorrow more!

IV

It was early morning. Everything had been made ready for the journey in Abraham's house. Abraham took leave of Sarah, and the faithful servant Eleazar followed him out on the way until he had to turn back. They rode together in accord, Abraham and Isaac, until they came to the mountain in Moriah. Yet Abraham made everything ready for the sacrifice, calmly and quietly, but as he turned away Isaac saw that Abraham's left hand was clenched in anguish, that a shudder went through his body – but Abraham drew the knife.

Then they turned home again and Sarah ran to meet them, but Isaac had lost his faith. Never a word in the whole world is spoken of this, and Isaac told no one what he had seen, and Abraham never suspected that anyone had seen it.

*

When the child is to be weaned the mother has more solid food at hand, so that the child will not perish. Lucky the one who has more solid food at hand!

In these and similar ways this man of whom we speak thought about those events. Every time he came home from a journey to the mountain in Moriah he collapsed in weariness, clasped his hands, and said: 'Yet no one was as great as Abraham; who is able to understand him?'

Speech in Praise of Abraham

If there were no eternal consciousness in a man, if at the bottom of everything there were only a wild ferment, a power that twisting in dark passions produced everything great or inconsequential; if an unfathomable, insatiable emptiness lay hid beneath everything, what would life be but despair? If it were thus, if there were no sacred bond uniting mankind, if one generation rose up after another like the leaves of the forest, if one generation succeeded the other as the songs of birds in the woods, if the human race passed through the world as a ship through the sea or the wind through the desert, a thoughtless and fruitless whim, if an eternal oblivion always lurked hungrily for its prey and there were no power strong enough to wrest it from its clutches – how empty and devoid of comfort would life be! But for that reason it is not so, and as God created man and woman, so too he shaped the hero and the poet or speech-maker. The latter has none of the skills of the former, he can only admire, love, take pleasure in the hero. Yet he, too, no less than the hero, is happy; for the hero is so to speak that better nature of his in which he is enamoured, though happy that it is not himself, that his love can indeed be admiration. He is the spirit of remembrance, can only bring to mind what has been done, do nothing but admire what has been done. He takes nothing of himself, but is jealous of his charge. He follows his heart's desire, but having found what he sought he wanders round to everyone's door with his song and his speech, so that all can admire the hero as he does, be proud of the hero as he is. That is his achievement, his humble task, this his faithful service in the hero's house. If he remains thus true to his love, if he struggles night and day against the wiles of oblivion, which would cheat him of his hero, then he has fulfilled his task, he is united with the hero who in his turn has loved him just as faithfully, for the poet is so to speak the *hero's* better nature, ineffectual certainly as a memory is, but also transfigured as a memory is. Therefore no one who was great will be forgotten: and however long it takes, even if a cloud of misunderstanding should take the hero away, his lover still comes, and the more time goes by the more faithfully he sticks by him.

No! No one shall be forgotten who was great in this world; but everyone was great in his own way, and everyone in proportion to the greatness of what *he loved*. For he who loved himself became great in himself, and he who loved others became great through his devotion, but he who loved God became greater than all. They shall all be remembered, but everyone became great in proportion to his *expectancy*. One became great through expecting the possible, another by expecting the eternal; but he who expected the impossible became greater than all. They shall all be remembered, but everyone was great in proportion to the magnitude of what he *strove with*. For he who strove with the world became great by conquering the world, and he who strove with himself became greater by conquering himself; but he who strove with God became greater than all. Thus there was strife in the world, man against man, one against thousands, but he who strove with God was greater than all. Thus there was strife upon earth: there was he who conquered everything by his own strength, and he who conquered God by his powerlessness. There was one who relied upon himself and gained everything, and one who, secure in his own strength, sacrificed everything; but greater than all was the one who believed God. There was one who was great in his strength, and one who was great in his wisdom, and one who was great in hope, and one who was great in love; but greater than all was Abraham, great with that power whose strength is powerlessness, great in that wisdom whose secret is folly, great in that hope whose outward form is insanity, great in that love which is hatred of self.

It was by his faith that Abraham could leave the land of his fathers to become a stranger in the land of promise. He left one thing behind, took another with him. He left behind his worldly understanding and took with him his faith. Otherwise he would surely not have gone; certainly it would have been senseless to do so. It was by his faith that he could be a stranger in the promised land; there was nothing to remind him of what was dear, but the novelty of everything tempted his soul to sad longing. And yet he was God's chosen, in whom the Lord was well pleased! Yes, indeed! If only he had been disowned, cast out from God's grace, he would have understood it better. As it was it looked more like a mockery of himself and his faith. There was once another who lived in exile from the beloved land of his fathers. He is not forgotten, nor his songs of lament in which in sorrow he sought and found what he had lost. From Abraham we have no song of lament. It is human to complain, human to weep with one who weeps, but it is greater to have faith and more blessed to behold the believer.

It was faith that made Abraham accept the promise that all nations of the earth should be blessed in his seed. Time went by, the possibility was still there, and Abraham had faith; time went by, it became unlikely, and Abraham had faith. There was once another who held out an expectation. Time went by, the evening drew near, he was not so pitiful as to forget his expectation; therefore he too should not be forgotten. Then he sorrowed, and the sorrow did not deceive him as life had done; it did all it could for him and in the sweetness of sorrow he possessed his disappointed expectation. It is human to sorrow with the sorrower, but greater to have faith and more blessed to behold the believer. From Abraham we have no song of sorrow. As time went by he did not mournfully count the days, he did not cast suspicious glances at Sarah, fearing she was growing old; he did not stay the march of the sun, so that Sarah should not grow old and with her his expectation; he did not soothingly sing to Sarah his mournful lay. Abraham became old and Sarah was mocked in the land, and still he was God's chosen and heir to the promise that in his seed all nations of the earth would be blessed. Would it not be better, then, were he not God's chosen? What is it to be God's chosen? Is it to be denied in youth one's youthful desire in order to have it fulfilled in great travail in old age? But Abraham believed and held firm to the promise. Had Abraham wavered he would have renounced it. He would have said to God: 'So perhaps after all it is not your will that it should happen; then I will give up my desire, it was my only desire, my blessed joy. My soul is upright, I bear no secret grudge because you refused it.' He would not have been forgotten, he would have saved many by his example, yet he would not have become the father of faith; for it is great to give up one's desire, but greater to stick to it after having given it up; it is great to grasp hold of the eternal but greater to stick to the temporal after having given it up. But then came the fullness of time. Had Abraham not had faith, then Sarah would surely have died of sorrow, and Abraham, dull with grief, instead of understanding the fulfilment, would have smiled at it as at a youthful dream. But Abraham believed, and therefore he *was* young; for he who always hopes for the best becomes old, deceived by life, and he who is always prepared for the worst becomes old prematurely; but he who has faith, retains eternal youth. All praise then to that tale! For Sarah, though stricken in years, was young enough to covet the pleasure of motherhood; and Abraham, though grey of head, was young enough to want to be a father. Outwardly the wonder of faith is in Abraham and Sarah's being young enough for it to happen according to their expectations; in a deeper sense the wonder of faith lies in Abraham and Sarah's being young enough to wish, and in faith's having preserved their wish and through it their youthfulness. He accepted the fulfilment of the promise, he accepted it in faith, and it happened according to expectation and according to faith; for Moses struck the rock with his rod but he did not believe.

So there was rejoicing in Abraham's house when Sarah was bride on their golden-wedding day.

But it was not to remain so; Abraham was to be tried once more. He had fought with that subtle power that invents everything, with that watchful opponent that never takes a nap, with that old man who outlives everything – time itself. He had fought with it and kept his faith. Now all the horrors of the struggle were to be concentrated in one moment. 'And God did tempt Abraham, and said unto him . . . Take now thy son, thine only son Isaac, whom thou lovest, and get thee into the land of Moriah; and offer him there for a burnt offering upon one of the mountains which I will tell thee of.'

So all was lost, more terrible than if it had never been! So the Lord was only making sport of Abraham! Through a miracle he had made the preposterous come true, now he would see it again brought to nothing. Foolery indeed! But Abraham did not laugh at it, as Sarah had laughed when the promise had first been proclaimed. All was lost! Seventy years' faithful expectation, the brief joy at faith's fulfilment. Who is it then that snatches the staff from the old man, who is it that demands that the old man himself should break it? Who is it that makes a man's grey hairs forlorn, who is it that demands that he himself should make them so? Is there no compassion for this venerable greybeard, none for the innocent child? And yet Abraham was God's chosen, and it was the Lord who put him to this test. All was now surely lost! The glorious memory of the human race, the promise in

Abraham's seed, it was only a whim, a fleeting thought of the Lord's, which Abraham himself must now eradicate. That glorious treasure, as old as the faith in Abraham's heart, many many years older than Isaac, the fruit of Abraham's life, hallowed with prayers, ripened in struggle – the blessing on Abraham's lips, this fruit was now to be plucked out of season and have no meaning; for what meaning could there be in it if Isaac was to be sacrificed! That sad yet still blessed hour when Abraham should take leave of everything he held dear, when he should raise his venerable head one time more, when his countenance should be radiant as the Lord's, when he should concentrate his whole soul in a blessing with the power to give Isaac joy all his days – that moment was not to come! For, yes, Abraham would indeed take leave of Isaac, but it was he that was to remain; death would divide them, but Isaac was to be its victim. The old man was not to lay his hand upon Isaac in blessing, but weary of life was to lay it upon him in violence. And it was God who tried him. Yes. Woe, woe to the messenger who came before Abraham with such tidings! Who would have dared be the emissary of such sorrow? Yet it was God who tried Abraham.

But Abraham had faith, and had faith for *this* life. Yes, had his faith only been for a future life it would indeed have been easier to cast everything aside in order to hasten out of this world to which he did not belong. But Abraham's faith was not of that kind, if there is such, for a faith like that is not really faith but only its remotest possibility, a faith that has some inkling of its object at the very edge of the field of vision but remains separated from it by a yawning abyss in which despair plays its pranks. But it was for this life that Abraham believed, he believed he would become old in his land, honoured among his people, blessed in his kin, eternally remembered in Isaac, the dearest in his life, whom he embraced with a love for which it was but a poor expression to say that he faithfully fulfilled the father's duty to love the son, as indeed the summons put it: 'the son whom thou lovest.' Jacob had twelve sons and he loved one; Abraham had just one, the son he loved.

But Abraham had faith and did not doubt. He believed the ridiculous. If Abraham had doubted – then he would have done something else, something great and glorious; for how could Abraham have done other than what is great and glorious? He would have marched out to the mountain in Moriah, chopped the firewood, set light to the fire, drawn the knife – he would have cried out to God: 'Do not scorn this sacrifice, it is not the best I possess, that I well know; for what is an old man compared with the child of promise, but it is the best I can give. Let Isaac never come to know, that he may comfort himself in his young years.' He would have thrust the knife into his own breast. He would have been admired in the world and his name never forgotten; but it is one thing to be admired, another to be a guiding star that saves the anguished.

But Abraham had faith. He did not beg for himself in hope of moving the Lord; it was only that time when the just punishment had been proclaimed upon Sodom and Gomorrah that Abraham came forward with his prayers.

We read in those Holy Scriptures: 'And God did tempt Abraham, and said unto him, Abraham: Abraham, where are you? but Abraham answered: here I am.' You, to whom my speech is addressed, was that the case with you? When you saw, far off, the heavy fate approaching, did you not say to the mountains, 'hide me', to the hills, 'fall on me'? Or if you were stronger, did your feet nevertheless not drag along the way? Did they not hanker, as it were, to get back into the old tracks? When you were called, did you answer, or did you not? Perhaps softly and in a whisper? Not so Abraham, gladly, boldly, trustingly he answered out loud 'here I am'. We read further: 'And Abraham rode up early in the morning.' He hurried as though to some celebration, and he was at the appointed place, the mountain in Moriah, early in the morning. He said nothing to Sarah, nothing to Elea-zar. After all, who could have understood him? Hadn't the test by its very nature exacted an oath of silence from him? 'And [he] clave the wood, he bound Isaac, he kindled the fire, he drew the knife.' My hearer! Many a father has felt the loss of his child as the loss of the dearest thing he has in the world, to be bereft of every hope for the future; yet no son was the child of promise in the sense that Isaac was for Abraham. Many a father has lost his child, but then it was God, the unchangeable and inscrutable will of the Almighty, it was his hand that took it. Not so with Abraham. For him a harder trial was reserved; along with the knife the fate of Isaac was put into Abraham's own hand. And he stood there, the old man with his only hope! But he did not doubt, he did not look in anguish to left or right, he did not challenge heaven with his prayers. He knew it was God the Almighty that tried him, he knew it was the hardest sacrifice that could be demanded of him; but he also knew that no sacrifice was too hard when God demanded it – and he drew the knife.

Who gave strength to Abraham's arm, who kept his right arm raised so that it did not fall helplessly down! Anyone who saw this would be paralysed. Who gave strength to Abraham's soul, so that his eye did not become too clouded to see either Isaac or the ram! Anyone who saw this would become blind. And yet rare enough though they may be, those who are both paralysed and blind, still more rare is he who can tell the story and give it its due. We know it, all of us – it was only a trial.

Had Abraham doubted as he stood on the mountain in Moriah, had he looked about in indecision, if before drawing the knife he had accidentally caught sight of the ram and God had allowed him to offer it in place of Isaac – then he would have gone home, everything would have been as before, he would have had Sarah, he would have kept Isaac, and yet how changed! For his withdrawal would have been a flight, his deliverance an accident, his reward dishonour, his future perhaps damnation. Then he would have borne witness, not to his faith or to God's mercy, but to how dreadful was the journey to the mountain in Moriah. Abraham would not be forgotten, nor the mountain. Yet it would not be mentioned like Ararat, where the Ark came to land, but as a horror, for it was here that Abraham doubted.

Venerable Father Abraham! When you journeyed

home from the mountain in Moriah you needed no speech of praise to console you for what was lost; for in fact you gained everything and kept Isaac. Was it not so? The Lord never again took him from you, you sat happily at table with him in your tent, as you do in the hereafter in all eternity. Venerable Father Abraham! Thousands of years have slipped by since those days, but you need no late-coming lover to snatch your memory from the power of oblivion; for every mother-tongue commemorates you – and still you reward your lover more gloriously than anyone. You make him blessed hereafter in your bosom, you captivate his eye and his heart in the here and now with the marvel of your deed. Venerable Father Abraham! Second father to the human race! You who first saw and bore witness to that tremendous passion that scorns the fearful struggle with the raging elements and the forces of creation in order to struggle with God instead, you who first knew that supreme passion, the sacred, pure, and humble expression of the divine madness which the pagans admired – forgive him who would speak in your praise if he did not do it correctly. He spoke humbly, seeing it is his heart's desire; he spoke briefly, as is fitting; but he will never forget that you needed a hundred years to get the son of your old age, against every expectation, that you had to draw the knife before keeping Isaac; he will never forget that in one hundred and thirty years you got no further than faith.

Problemata

Preamble from the Heart

An old proverb pertaining to the outward and visible world says: 'Only one who works gets bread.' Oddly enough, the saying doesn't apply in the world to which it most properly belongs, for the outward world is subject to the law of imperfection; there it happens time and again that one who gets bread is one who does not work, that one who sleeps gets it in greater abundance than one who labours. In the outward world everything belongs to whoever has it, the outward world is subject to the law of indifference and the genie of the ring obeys the one who wears it, whether he be a Noureddin or an Aladdin, and whoever holds the world's treasures does so however he came by them. It is otherwise in the world of spirit. Here there prevails an eternal divine order, here it does not rain on the just and the unjust alike, here the sun does not shine on both good and evil, here only one who works gets bread, and only one who knows anguish finds rest, only one who descends to the underworld saves the loved one, only one who draws the knife gets Isaac. He who will not work does not get bread, but will be deluded, as the gods deluded Orpheus with an airy figure in place of the beloved, deluded him because he was tender-hearted, not courageous, deluded him because he was a lyre-player, not a man.

Here it is no help to have Abraham as one's father, or

seventeen centuries of noble ancestry; of anyone who will not work here one can say what is written about Israel's virgins, he gives birth to wind – while the one who works will give birth to his own father.

Conventional wisdom aims presumptuously to introduce into the world of spirit that same law of indifference under which the outside world groans. It believes it is enough to have knowledge of large truths. No other work is necessary. But then it does not get bread, it starves to death while everything is transformed into gold. And what else does it know? There were many thousands in the Greece of the time, countless others in later generations, who knew all the victories of Miltiades, but there was only one who lost sleep over them. There were countless generations that knew the story of Abraham by heart, word for word. How many did it make sleepless?

Now the story of Abraham has the remarkable quality that it will always be glorious no matter how impoverished our understanding of it, but only – for it is true here too – if we are willing to 'labour and be heavy laden'. But labour they will not, and yet they still want to understand the story. One speaks in Abraham's honour, but how? By making it a commonplace: 'his greatness was that he so loved God that he was willing to offer him the best he had.' That is very true, but 'best' is a vague expression. In word and thought one can quite safely identify Isaac with the best, and the man who so thinks can very well puff at his pipe as he does so, and the listener can very well leisurely stretch out his legs. If the rich young man whom Christ met on the road had sold all his possessions and given them to the poor, we would praise him as we praise all great deeds, but we would not understand even him without some labour. Yet he would not have become an Abraham even had he given away the best he had. What is left out of the Abraham story is the anguish; for while I am under no obligation to money, to a son the father has the highest and most sacred of obligations. Yet anguish is a dangerous affair for the squeamish, so people forget it, notwithstanding they want to talk about Abraham. So they talk and in the course of conversation they interchange the words 'Isaac' and 'best'. Everything goes excellently. Should someone in the audience be suffering from insomnia, however, there is likely to be the most appalling, most profound, tragi-comic misunderstanding. He goes home, he wants to do just like Abraham; for the son is certainly the best thing he has. Should that speaker hear word of this, he might go to the man, summon all his clerical authority, and shout: 'Loathsome man, dregs of society, what devil has so possessed you that you wanted to murder your own son?' And this priest, who had felt no signs of heat or perspiration while preaching about Abraham, would be surprised at the righteous wrath with which he fulminates against that poor man; he would be pleased with himself, for never had he spoken with such pungency and fervour before. He would say to himself, and his wife: 'I'm an orator, all I've needed was the opportunity; when I spoke about Abraham on Sunday I didn't feel at all carried away.' If the same speaker still had some slight excess of wit to spare he would surely lose it were the sinner to reply

coolly and with dignity: 'It was in fact what you yourself
preached on Sunday.' How could a priest get such an
idea into his head? And yet he did so, and the mistake
was only that he hadn't known what he was saying. Why
doesn't some poet take up situations like these instead
of the stuff and nonsense that fills comedies and novels?
The comic and the tragic converge on each other here
in absolute infinity. The priest's speech was no doubt
laughable enough in itself, but became infinitely more
so in its consequence, and yet that was quite natural. Or
suppose the sinner had acceded without protest to the
priest's reprimand; or that zealous cleric had gone happily home, happy in the knowledge that his effectiveness
was not confined to the pulpit but was above all evident
in the irresistible power of his ministry to souls, inspiring
the congregation on Sunday while on Monday, like a
cherub with flaming sword, confronting him who by his
deed would put that old proverb to shame which says
that the world never practises what the priest preaches.*

Should the sinner, on the other hand, not be convinced, his situation would be tragic enough. He would
no doubt be executed or sent to the madhouse; in short
he would have come into an unhappy relation to so-
called reality, though in another sense I should think that

---

* In olden days people said, 'What a shame things in the world don't
go in the way the priest preaches.' But the time may be coming, not
least with the help of philosophy, when we shall be able to say, 'How
fortunate that things in the world don't go in the way the priest
preaches, since at least there's a little meaning to life, but none in his
sermon.'

Abraham made him happy: for he who labours does not perish.

What explains a contradiction like this speaker's? Is it because Abraham has acquired proprietary rights to the title of great man, so that whatever he does is great, and if anyone else does the same it is a sin, a crying sin? If so, I have no wish to take part in such mindless praise. If faith cannot make it into a holy deed to murder one's own son, then let the judgement fall on Abraham as on anyone else. If one hasn't the courage to think this thought through, to say that Abraham was a murderer, then surely it is better to acquire that courage than to waste time on undeserved speeches in his praise. The ethical expression for what Abraham did is that he was willing to murder Isaac; the religious expression is that he was willing to sacrifice Isaac; but in this contradiction lies the very anguish that can indeed make one sleepless; and yet without that anguish Abraham is not the one he is. Or perhaps Abraham simply didn't do what the story says, perhaps in the context of his times what he did was something quite different. Then let's forget him, for why bother remembering a past that cannot be made into a present? Or perhaps something to do with the ethical aspect slipped that speaker's mind, the fact that Isaac was the son. For if you simply remove faith as a nix and nought there remains only the raw fact that Abraham was willing to murder Isaac, which is easy enough for anyone without faith to imitate; without the faith, that is, which makes it hard.

For my own part I don't lack the courage to think a thought whole. No thought has frightened me so far.

Should I ever come across one I hope I will at least have the honesty to say: 'This thought scares me, it stirs up something else in me so that I don't want to think it.' If that is wrong of me I'll no doubt get my punishment. If I had conceded the truth of the judgement that Abraham was a murderer, I am not sure that I would have been able to silence my reverence of him. But if that is what I myself thought, then I would presumably keep quiet, for thoughts like that are not to be intimated to others. However, Abraham is no illusion; he hasn't slept himself to fame; he does not owe his celebrity to any whim of fate.

Can one speak unreservedly of Abraham, then, without risking that someone will go off the rails and do likewise? Unless I dare to speak quite openly I will simply keep quiet about Abraham, and above all not diminish him so that by that very fact he becomes a snare for the weak. If one makes faith the main thing – that is, makes it what it is – then I imagine one might dare speak of it without that risk in this day of ours which can hardly be said to outdo itself in faith, and it is only in respect of faith that one achieves resemblance to Abraham, not murder. If one makes love into a fleeting mood, into a pleasurable agitation in a person, then one lays traps for the weak when talking of the achievements of love. Of course everyone has momentary feelings, but if those were to be used as reasons for doing the terrible things that love has hallowed as immortal deeds everything would be lost, both the achievement and those misled in this way.

It should be all right, then, to speak about Abraham.

The great can never do harm when grasped in their greatness. It is like a two-edged sword, bringing death and salvation. If it should fall to my lot to speak of him, I would begin by showing what a devout and God-fearing man Abraham was, deserving to be called God's chosen. Only such a person is subjected to such a trial; but who is such a person? Next I would describe how Abraham loved Isaac. To that end I would beg the support of all good spirits in making my speech as fervent as is the love of a father for his son. I would hope to describe it in such a way that not many a father in the realm would dare maintain that he loved his son thus. Yet if he did not love as Abraham, all thought of offering Isaac would be a temptation. Here we already have plenty to speak of for several Sundays, so there is no need to rush. The result, if the speech does justice to the theme, will be that some fathers will simply not want to hear more, but be happy for the time being if they have really succeeded in loving as Abraham did. Should one of them after having caught the greatness of Abraham's deed, but also the appallingness of it, venture out on the road, I would saddle my horse and ride along with him. At every stop before we came to the mountain in Moriah I would explain to him that he could still turn back, could rue the misunderstanding that he was called to be tried in a conflict of this nature, could confess that he lacked the courage, so that if God wanted Isaac God must take him himself. It is my conviction that such a person will not be disavowed, but can be blessed along with all others, though not in time. Even in times of faith would such a person not be judged in this way? I knew someone who once could have saved my life had he possessed magnanimity. He said plainly: 'I see well enough what I could do, but I don't dare. I'm afraid that later I shall lack strength, that I shall regret it.' He was not magnanimous, but would anyone cease to love him on that account?

Having spoken thus, and moved my audience so that they appreciated at least something of the dialectical struggle of faith and its gigantic passion, I would not be guilty of the error they might impute to me by thinking: 'Well, he has faith in such a high degree it's enough for us just to hold on to his coat-tails.' For I would add: 'By no means have I faith. I am a shrewd fellow by nature, such as always have great difficulty making the movement of faith, though I wouldn't attach *any importance in itself to a difficulty which, by overcoming it, brings a shrewd fellow no further than the most ordinary and simple-minded person has already reached without the difficulty.'*

Love, after all, has its priests in the poets, and occasionally one hears a voice that knows how to keep it in shape; but about faith one hears not a word, who speaks in *this* passion's praises? Philosophy goes further. Theology sits all painted at the window courting philosophy's favour, offering philosophy its delights. It is said to be hard to understand Hegel, while understanding Abraham, why, that's a bagatelle. To go beyond Hegel, that is a miracle, but to go beyond Abraham is the simplest of all. I for my part have devoted considerable time to understanding the Hegelian philosophy, believe also that I have more or less understood it, am rash enough to believe that at those points where, despite the trouble taken, I cannot understand it, the reason is that Hegel himself hasn't been altogether clear. All this I do easily, naturally, without it causing me any mental strain. But when I have to think about Abraham I am virtually annihilated. I am all the time aware of that monstrous paradox that is the content of Abraham's life. I am constantly repulsed, and my thought, for all its passion, is unable to enter into it, cannot come one hairbreadth further. I strain every muscle to catch sight of it, but the same instant I become paralysed.

I am not unacquainted with what has been admired as great and magnanimous in the world; my soul feels an affinity with it, and is in all humility convinced that it was in my cause too that the hero strove; as I contemplate his striving I exclaim to myself: *'Jam tua res agitur'* [Now it's your affair that's at stake]. The hero I can *think* myself *into*, but not Abraham; when I reach that height I fall down since what I'm offered is a paradox. Yet I by no means think that faith is therefore something inferior, on the contrary that it is the highest, at the same time believing it dishonest of philosophy to offer something else instead and to slight faith. Philosophy cannot and should not give us an account of faith, but should understand itself and know just what it has indeed to offer, without taking anything away, least of all cheating people out of something by making them think it is nothing. I am not unacquainted with life's needs and dangers, I do not fear them, and I go to meet them undaunted. I am not unfamiliar with horror, my memory is a faithful wife and my imagination, unlike myself, a diligent maid who sits quietly all day at her work and in the evening can speak so prettily for me that I just have to look at it even if it isn't always landscapes or flowers or pastoral idylls she paints. I have seen horror face to face, I do not flee it in fear but know very well that, however bravely I face it, my courage is not that of faith and not at all to be compared with it. I cannot close my eyes and hurl myself trustingly into the absurd, for me it is impossible, but I do not praise myself on that account. I am convinced that God is love; this thought has for me a pristine lyrical validity. When it is present to me I am unspeakably happy, when it is absent I yearn for it more intensely than the lover for the beloved; but I do not have faith, this courage I lack. God's love is for me, both in a direct and inverse sense, incommensurable with the whole of reality. I am not coward enough to whimper and moan on that account, but neither am I underhand enough to deny that faith is something far higher. I can very well carry on living in my manner, I am happy and satisfied, but my happiness is not that of faith and compared with that is indeed unhappy. I do not burden God with my petty cares, details don't concern me, I gaze only upon my love and keep its virginal flame pure and clear; faith is convinced that God troubles himself about the smallest thing. In this life I am content to be wedded to the left hand, faith is humble enough to demand the right; and that it is indeed humility I don't, and shall never, deny.

But I wonder whether all my contemporaries really are capable of making the movement of faith? Unless I am much mistaken they are more inclined to pride themselves for doing what they don't even think me capable of, i.e. the imperfect. It is against my nature to do what people so often do, talk inhumanly about the great as though some thousands of years were a huge distance; I prefer to talk about it humanly as though it happened yesterday and let only the greatness itself be the distance that either exalts or condemns. If – *in the guise of tragic hero*, for higher than that I cannot come – I were summoned to such an extraordinary royal progress as that to the mountain in Moriah I know very well what I would have done. I would not have been coward enough to stay at home, nor would I have rested on the way or dawdled, or forgotten the knife to create some delay; I am fairly certain I would have been there on the dot, with everything arranged – I might even have come too early instead, so as to have done with it quickly. But I also know what else I would have done. The moment I mounted the horse I would have said to myself: 'Now everything is lost, God demands Isaac, I sacrifice him, and with him all my joy – yet God is love and for me continues to be so.' For in the temporal world God and I cannot talk together, we have no common language. Perhaps someone or other in our time would be foolish enough, envious enough of the great, to want to suppose, and have me suppose, that had I actually done this I would have done something even greater than Abraham, for wouldn't my immense resignation be far more idealistic and poetic than Abraham's narrow-mindedness? And yet this is the greatest falsehood, for my immense resignation would be a substitute for faith. Nor could I have made more than the infinite movement in order to find myself again and rest once more in myself. Neither would I have loved Isaac as Abraham did. The fact that

I made the movement resolutely might demonstrate my courage humanly speaking, that I loved him with all my soul is a precondition without which the whole affair becomes an act of wickedness, and yet I would not have loved as Abraham loved; for then I would have held back at the very last minute, though without this meaning that I'd arrive late at the mountain in Moriah. Furthermore my behaviour would have vitiated the whole story, for I would have been at a loss had I got Isaac back again. What Abraham found the easiest of all would for me be hard, to find joy again in Isaac! For he who with all the infinity of his soul, *proprio motu et propriis auspiciis* [on his own accord and on his own responsibility], has made the infinite movement and can do no more, that person only keeps Isaac with pain.

But what did Abraham do? He came neither too *early* nor too late. He mounted the ass, he rode slowly down the path. All along he had faith, he believed that God would not demand Isaac of him, while still he was willing to offer him if that was indeed what was demanded. He believed on the strength of the absurd, for there could be no question of human calculation, and it was indeed absurd that God who demanded this of him should in the next instant withdraw the demand. He climbed the mountain, even in that moment when the knife gleamed he believed – that God would not demand Isaac. Certainly he was surprised by the outcome, but by means of a double movement he had come back to his original position and therefore received Isaac more joyfully than the first time. Let us go further. We let Isaac actually be sacrificed. Abraham had faith. His faith was not that he should be happy sometime in the hereafter, but that he should find blessed happiness here in this world. God could give him a new Isaac, bring the sacrificial offer back to life. He believed on the strength of the absurd, for all human calculation had long since been suspended. That sorrow can make one demented may be granted and is hard enough; that there is a strength of will that hauls close enough to the wind to save the understanding, even if the strain turns one slightly odd, that too may be granted. I don't mean to decry that. But to be able to lose one's understanding and with it the whole of the finite world whose stockbroker it is, and then on the strength of the absurd get exactly the same finitude back again, that leaves me aghast. But I don't say on that account that it is of little worth; on the contrary it is the one and only marvel. It is commonly supposed that what faith produces is no work of art but a crude and vulgar effort only for clumsier natures; yet the truth is quite otherwise. The dialectic of faith is the most refined and most remarkable of all dialectics, it has an elevation that I can form a conception of but no more. I can make the great trampoline leap in which I pass over into infinitude, my back is like the tight-rope walker's, twisted in my childhood, and so it is easy for me. One, two, three, I can go upside down in existence, but the next is beyond me, for the marvel I cannot perform but only be amazed at. Yes, if only Abraham, the instant he swung his leg over the ass's back, had said to himself: 'Now Isaac is lost, I could just as well sacrifice him here at home as journey the long road to Moriah' – then I wouldn't need Abraham, whereas now I bow to his name seven times and to his deed seventy. For that is not what he did, as I can prove by the fact that he received Isaac back with joy, really heartfelt joy, that he needed no preparation, no time to adjust himself to finitude and its joy. Had it not been thus with Abraham he may well have loved God, but he would not have had faith; for he who loves God without faith reflects on himself, while the person who loves God reflects on God.

At this extremity stands Abraham. The last stage he loses sight of is infinite resignation. He really does go further and comes *to* faith, for all these caricatures of faith, the pitiable, lukewarm apathy that thinks 'There's surely no need, it's not worth worrying before the time', the miserable hope that says 'Who knows what may happen, it's possible certainly' – these distortions belong to life's wretchedness, and these infinite resignation has already infinitely scorned.

Abraham I cannot understand; in a way all I can learn from him is to be amazed. If one imagines one can be moved to faith by considering the outcome of this story, one deceives oneself, and is out to cheat God of faith's first movement, one is out to suck the life-wisdom out of the paradox. One or another may succeed, for our age does not stop with faith, with its miracle of turning water into wine; it goes further, it turns wine into water.

Would it not be best all the same to stop with faith, and is it not disturbing that everyone wants to go further? When people nowadays – as is in fact variously announced – will not stop with love, where is it they are going? To worldly wisdom, petty calculation, to paltriness and misery, to all that can put man's divine origin in doubt?

Would it not be better to remain standing at faith, and for the one who stands there to take care not to fall? For the movement of faith must be made continually on the strength of the absurd, though in such a way, be it noted, that one does not lose finitude but gains it all of a piece. I for my part can indeed describe the movements of faith, but I cannot perform them. When learning how to make swimming movements, one can hang in a belt from the ceiling; one may be said to describe the movements all right but one isn't swimming; likewise I can describe the movements of faith but when I am thrown into the water, although I may be said to be swimming (for I'm not among the waders), I make other movements, I make the movements of infinity, while faith does the opposite, having performed the movements of infinity it makes those of finitude. Lucky the one who can make those movements, he performs a marvel, and I shall never tire of admiring him. Whether it is Abraham or the servant in Abraham's house, whether a professor of philosophy or a poor serving-maid is for me absolutely immaterial, I look only at the movements. But those I do indeed look at and let myself be fooled neither by myself nor by anyone else. The knights of infinite resignation are readily recognizable, their gait is gliding, bold. But those who wear the jewel of faith can easily disappoint, for their exterior bears a remarkable similarity to what infinite resignation itself as much as faith scorns, namely the *bourgeois* philistine.

In my own experience I frankly admit to having found no reliable examples, though I would not deny on that ground that possibly every other person is one. Still, I have tried now in vain for several years to track one down. People commonly travel the world over to see rivers and mountains, new stars, garish birds, freak fish, grotesque breeds of human; they fall into an animal stupor that gapes at existence and they think they have seen something. I am not concerned with this. But if I knew where such a knight of faith lived I would journey to him on foot, for this marvel concerns me absolutely. I would not let him slip one instant, but watch every minute how he makes the movements; I would consider myself maintained for life and divide my time between looking at him and practising the movements myself, thus devoting *all* my time to admiring him. As I said, I haven't found such a one; still, I can very well imagine him. Here he is. The acquaintance is struck, I am introduced. The moment I first set eyes on him I thrust him away, jump back, clasp my hands together and say half aloud: 'Good God! Is this the person, is it really him? He looks just like a tax-gatherer.' Yet it is indeed him. I come a little closer, watch the least movement in case some small, incongruous optical telegraphic message from the infinite should appear, a glance, expression, gesture, a sadness, a smile betraying the infinite by its incongruity with the finite. No! I examine him from top to toe, in case there should be some crack through which the infinite peeped out. No! He is solid through and through. His stance? Vigorous, it belongs altogether to finitude, no smartly turned-out townsman taking a stroll out to Fresberg on a Sunday afternoon treads the ground with surer foot; he belongs altogether to the world, no *petit bourgeois* belongs to it more. One detects nothing of the strangeness and superiority that mark the knight of the infinite. This man takes pleasure, takes part, in everything, and whenever one catches him occupied with something his engagement has the persistence of the worldly person whose soul is wrapped up in such things. He minds his affairs. To see him at them you would think he was some pen-pusher who had lost his soul to Italian book-keeping, so attentive to detail is he. He takes a holiday on Sundays. He goes to church. No heavenly glance or any other sign of the incommensurable betrays him; if one didn't know him it would be impossible to set him apart from the rest of the crowd; for at most his hearty, lusty psalm-singing proves that he has a good set of lungs. In the afternoon he takes a walk in the woods. He delights in everything he sees, in the thronging humanity, the new omnibuses, the Sound – to run across him on Strandveien you would think he was a shop-keeper having his fling, such is his way of taking pleasure; for he is not a poet and I have sought in vain to prise out of him the secret of any poetic incommensurability. Towards evening he goes home, his step tireless as a postman's. On the way it occurs to him that his wife will surely have some special little warm dish for his return, for example roast head of lamb with vegetables. If he were to meet a kindred spirit, he could continue as far as Østerport so as to converse with him about this dish with a passion befitting a *restaurateur*. As it happens he hasn't a penny and yet he firmly believes his wife has that delicacy waiting for him. If she has, to see him eat it would be a sight for superior people to envy and for plain folk to be inspired by, for his appetite is greater than Esau's. If his wife doesn't have the dish, curiously enough he is exactly the same. On the road he passes a building-site and meets another man. They talk together for a moment, he has a building raised in a jiffy, having all that's needed for that. The stranger leaves him thinking: 'That must have been a capitalist,' while my admirable knight thinks: 'Yes, if it came to that I could surely manage it.' He takes his ease at an open window and looks down on the square where he lives, at everything that goes on – a rat slipping under a board over the gutter, the children at play – with a composure befitting a sixteen-year-old girl. And yet he is no genius, I have tried in vain to spy out in him the incommensurability of the genius. He smokes his pipe in the evening: to see him you would swear it was the cheesemonger opposite vegetating in the dusk. Carefree as a devil-may-care good-for-nothing, he hasn't a worry in the world, and yet he purchases every moment that he lives, 'redeeming the seasonable time' at the dearest price; not the least thing does he do except on the strength of the absurd. And yet, and yet – yes, it could drive me to fury, out of envy if for no other reason – and yet this man has made and is at every moment making the movement of infinity. He drains in infinite resignation the deep sorrow of existence, he knows the bliss of infinity, he has felt the pain of renouncing everything, whatever is most precious in the world, and yet to him finitude tastes just as good as to one who has never known anything higher, for his remaining in the finite bore no trace of a stunted, anxious training, and still he has this sense of being secure to take pleasure in it, as though it were the most certain thing of all. And yet, and yet the whole earthly form he presents is a new creation on the strength of the absurd. He resigned everything infinitely, and then took everything back on the strength of the absurd. He is continually making the movement of infinity, but he makes it with such accuracy and poise that he is continually getting finitude out of it, and not for a second would one suspect anything else. It is said that the dancer's hardest task is to leap straight into a definite position, so that not for a second does he have to catch at the position but stands there in it in the leap itself. Perhaps no dancer can do it – but that knight does it. The mass of humans live disheartened lives of earthly sorrow and joy, these are the sitters-out who will not join in the dance. The knights of infinity are dancers too and they have elevation. They make the upward movement and fall down again, and this too is no unhappy pastime, nor ungracious to behold. But when they come down they cannot assume the position straightaway, they waver an instant and the wavering shows they are nevertheless strangers in the world. This may be more or less evident, depending on their skill, but even the most skilled of these knights cannot hide the vacillation. One doesn't need to see them in the air, one only has to see them the moment they come and have come to earth to recognize them. But to be able to land in just that way, and in the same second to look as though one was up and walking, to transform the leap in life to a gait, to express the sublime in the pedestrian absolutely – that is something only the knight of faith can do – and it is the one and only marvel.

Yet this marvel can so easily deceive. I will therefore

describe the movements in a particular case which can illustrate the respective relationships to reality, for it is these that everything turns on. A young lad falls in love with a princess, the content of his whole life lies in this love, and yet the relationship is one that cannot possibly be brought to fruition, be translated from ideality into reality.* The slaves of misery, the frogs in life's swamp, naturally exclaim: 'Such love is foolishness; the rich brewer's widow is just as good and sound a match.' Let them croak away undisturbed in the swamp. This is not the manner of the knight of infinite resignation, he does not renounce the love, not for all the glory in the world. He is no trifler. He first makes sure that this really is the content of his life, and his soul is too healthy and proud to squander the least thing on getting drunk. He is not cowardly, he is not afraid to let his love steal in upon his most secret, most hidden thoughts, to let it twine itself in countless coils around every ligament of his consciousness – if the love becomes unhappy he will never be able to wrench himself out of it. He feels a blissful rapture when he lets it tingle through every nerve, and yet his soul is as solemn as his who has emptied the cup of poison and feels the juice penetrate to every drop of blood – for this moment is life and death. Having thus

* Of course any other interest whatever in which an individual concentrates the whole of life's reality can, when it proves unrealizable, give rise to the movement of resignation. But I have chosen falling in love to illustrate the movements because this interest will no doubt be more readily understood and thus it relieves me of the need to make all the introductory comments which would be of direct interest to only a few.

imbibed all the love and absorbed himself in it, he does not lack the courage to attempt and risk everything. He reflects over his life's circumstances, he summons the swift thoughts that like trained doves obey his every signal, he waves his rod over them, and they rush off in all directions. But now when they all return as messengers of sorrow and explain to him that it is an impossibility, he becomes quiet, he dismisses them, he remains alone, and he performs the movement. If what I say here has any meaning the movement must take place properly.* For the knight will then, in the first place, have the strength to concentrate the whole of his life's content and the meaning of reality in a single wish. If a person lacks this concentration, this focus, his soul is disintegrated from the start, and then he will never come to make the movement, he will act prudently in life like those capitalists who invest their capital in every kind of security so as to gain on the one what they lose on the

---

* This requires passion. Every movement of infinity occurs with passion, and no reflection can bring about a movement. That's the perpetual leap in life which explains the movement, while mediation is a chimera which in Hegel is supposed to explain everything and besides is the only thing he has never tried to explain. Passion is needed even to make the familiar Socratic distinction between what one does and what one doesn't understand; naturally even more so in making the genuinely Socratic movement, that of ignorance. What we lack today is not reflection but passion. For that reason our age is really in a sense too tenacious of life to die, for dying is one of the most remarkable leaps, and a small verse has always greatly attracted me, because having wished himself all the good and simple things in life in five or six lines previously, the poet ends thus: 'ein seliger Sprung in die Ewigkeit' [a blessed leap into eternity].

other – in short, he is not a knight. Secondly, the knight will have the strength to concentrate the whole of the result of his reflection into one act of consciousness. If he lacks this focus his soul is disintegrated from the start and he will then never have time to make the movement, he will be forever running errands in life, never enter the eternal; for at the very moment he is almost there he will suddenly discover that he has forgotten something and so must go back. The next moment he will think it possible, and that is also quite correct; but through such considerations one never comes to make the movement; rather with their help one sinks ever deeper into the mire.

So the knight makes the movement, but what movement? Does he want to forget the whole thing? Because in that too there is a kind of concentration. No! for the knight does not contradict himself, and it is a contradiction to forget the whole of one's life's content and still be the same. He has no inclination to become another, seeing nothing at all great in that prospect. Only lower natures forget themselves and become something new. Thus the butterfly has altogether forgotten that it was a caterpillar, perhaps it can so completely forget in turn that it was a butterfly that it can become a fish. Deeper natures never forget themselves and never become something other than they were. So the knight will remember everything; but the memory is precisely the pain, and yet in his infinite resignation he is reconciled with existence. His love for the princess would take on for him the expression of an eternal love, would acquire a religious character, be transfigured into a love for the eternal being which, although it denied fulfilment, still reconciled him once more in the eternal consciousness of his love's validity in an eternal form that no reality can take from him. Fools and young people talk about everything being possible for a human being. But that is a great mistake. Everything is possible spiritually speaking, but in the finite world there is much that is not possible. This impossibility the knight nevertheless makes possible by his expressing it spiritually, but he expresses it spiritually by renouncing it. The desire which would convey him out into reality, but came to grief on an impossibility, now bends inwards but is not lost thereby nor forgotten. At times it is the unconscious workings of the desire in him which awaken the memory, at others it is he himself that awakens it, for he is too proud to want to let the whole content of his life seem to have been but a fleeting affair of the moment. He keeps this love young, and it grows with him in years and beauty. On the other hand, he needs no finite occasion for its growth. From the moment he made the movement the princess is lost. He needs none of this erotic titillation of the nerves at the sight of the loved one, etc., nor does he need in a finite sense to be continually making his farewell, for his memory of her is an eternal one, and he knows very well that those lovers who are so eager to see one another one more time to say farewell are right to be eager, right to think it will be the last time; for as soon as may be they will have forgotten one another. He has grasped the deep secret that even in loving another one should be sufficient unto oneself. He pays no further finite attention to what the princess does, and just this proves that he has made the movement infinitely. Here we have the opportunity to see whether the movement in the individual is proper or not. There was a person who also believed he had made the movement, but time went by, the princess did something else, she married, say, a prince, and his soul lost the resilience of resignation. He knew then that he had not made the movement correctly; for one who has infinitely resigned is enough unto himself. The knight does not cancel his resignation, he keeps it, just as young as in the first instance, he never lets it go, simply because he has made the movement infinitely. What the princess does cannot disturb him, it is only lower natures who have the law for their actions in someone else, the premises for their actions outside themselves. If, on the other hand, the princess is similarly disposed there will be a beautiful development. She will then introduce herself into that order of knighthood whose members are not admitted by ballot but which anyone can join who has the courage to admit him- or herself, that order of knighthood which proves its immortality by making no distinction between man and woman. She too will keep her love young and sound, she too will have overcome her agony, even though she does not, as the song says, 'lie by her lord's side'. These two will then be suited to each other in all eternity, with such a strict-tempoed *harmonia praestabilita* [pre-established harmony] that were some moment to come, a moment with which they were nevertheless not concerned finitely, for in the finite world they would grow old – were such a moment to come which allowed their love its expression in time, then they would be in a position to begin precisely where they would have begun had they been united from the beginning. The one, whether man or woman, who understands this can never be deceived, for it is only lower natures who imagine they are deceived. No girl who lacks this pride really knows what it is to love, but if she is so proud, then all the world's stratagems and ingenuity cannot deceive her.

In infinite resignation there is peace and repose; anyone who wants it, who has not debased himself by – what is still worse than being too proud – belittling himself, can discipline himself into making this movement, which in its pain reconciles one to existence. Infinite resignation is that shirt in the old fable. The thread is spun with tears, bleached by tears, the shirt sewn in tears, but then it also gives better protection than iron and steel. A defect of the fable is that a third party is able to make the material. The secret in life is that everyone must sew it for himself; and the remarkable thing is that a man can sew it just as well as a woman. In infinite resignation there is peace and repose and consolation in the pain, that is if the movement is made properly. I could easily fill a whole book with the various misunderstandings, awkward positions, and slovenly movements I have encountered in just my own slight experience. People believe very little in spirit, yet it is precisely spirit that is needed to make this movement; what matters is its not being a one-sided result of *dira necessitas*; the more it is that the more doubtful it always is that the movement is proper. To insist that a frigid, sterile necessity is necessarily present is to say that no one may experience death before actually dying, which strikes me as crass materialism. Yet in our time people are less concerned with making pure movements. Suppose someone wanting to learn to dance said: 'For hundreds of years now one generation after another has been learning dance steps, it's high time I took advantage of this and began straight off with a set of quadrilles.' One would surely laugh a little at him; but in the world of spirit such an attitude is considered utterly plausible. What then is education? I had thought it was the curriculum the individual ran through in order to catch up with himself; and anyone who does not want to go through this curriculum will be little helped by being born into the most enlightened age.

Infinite resignation is the last stage before faith, so that anyone who has not made this movement does not have faith; for only in infinite resignation does my eternal validity become transparent to me, and only then can there be talk of grasping existence on the strength of faith.

Let us now have the knight of faith make his appearance in the case discussed. He does exactly the same as the other knight, he infinitely renounces the claim to the love which is the content of his life; he is reconciled in pain; but then comes the marvel, he makes one more movement, more wonderful than anything else, for he says: 'I nevertheless believe that I shall get her, namely on the strength of the absurd, on the strength of the fact that for God all things are possible.' The absurd is not one distinction among others embraced by understanding. It is not the same as the improbable, the unexpected, the unforeseen. The moment the knight resigned he was convinced of the impossibility, humanly speaking; that was a conclusion of the understanding, and he had energy enough to think it. In an infinite sense, however, it was possible, through renouncing it [as a finite possibility]; but then accepting that [possibility] is at the same time to have given it up, yet for the understanding there is no absurdity in possessing it, for it is only in the finite world that understanding rules and there it was and remains an impossibility. On this the knight of faith is just as clear; all that can save him is the absurd; and this he grasps by faith. Accordingly he admits the impossibility and at the same time believes the absurd; for were he to suppose that he had faith without recognizing the impossibility with all the passion of his soul and with all his heart, he would be deceiving himself, and his testimony would carry weight nowhere, since he would not even have come as far as infinite resignation.

Faith is therefore no aesthetic emotion, but something far higher, exactly because it presupposes resignation; it is not the immediate inclination of the heart but the paradox of existence. Thus that a young girl in the face of all difficulties rests assured that her desire will be fulfilled in no way means that her certainty is that of faith, even if she has been brought up by Christian parents and perhaps gone for a whole year to the pastor. She is convinced in all her childlike simplicity and innocence. This assurance too ennobles her nature and gives her a preternatural dimension, so that like a worker of wonders she can charm the finite powers of existence and make even stones weep, while on the other hand in her distraction she can just as well run to Herod as to Pilate and move the whole world with her pleas. Her conviction is ever so lovable, and one can learn much from her, but one thing one does not learn from her, how to make movements. Her certainty does not dare look the impossibility in the eye in the pain of resignation.

I can see then that it requires strength and energy and freedom of spirit to make the infinite movement of resignation; I can also see that it can be done. The next step dumbfounds me, my brain reels; for having made the movement of resignation, now on the strength of the absurd to get everything, to get one's desire, whole, in full, that requires more-than-human powers, it is a marvel. But at least I can see this, that the young girl's conviction is mere frivolity compared with a faith that is unshakeable even when it sees the impossibility. Whenever I want to make this movement I turn giddy, at the same moment I admire it absolutely and yet in that same instant an immense anxiety seizes my soul, for what is it to test God? And yet this is the movement of faith and remains that, however much philosophy, in order to confuse concepts, will have us suppose that it has faith, however much theology wants to sell it at a bargain price.

Resignation does not require faith, for what I win in resignation is my eternal consciousness, and that is a purely philosophical movement, which I venture upon when necessary, and which I can discipline myself into doing, for every time something finite out-distances me I starve myself until I make the movement; for my eternal consciousness is my love of God, and for me that is higher than anything. Resignation does not require faith, but it requires faith to get the slightest more than my eternal consciousness, for that [more] is the paradox. The movements are often confused. It is said that faith is needed in order to renounce everything; yes, even more strangely one hears people complain that they have lost faith and on consulting the scale to see where they are, we find curiously enough that they have come no further than the point where they should be making the infinite movement of resignation. Through resignation I renounce everything, this movement is one I do by myself, and when I do not do it that is because I am cowardly and weak and lack the enthusiasm and have no sense of the importance of the high dignity afforded to every human being, to be his own censor, a dignity greater by far than to be Censor General for the whole Roman Republic. This movement is one that I make by myself, so what I win is myself in my eternal consciousness, in a blessed compliance with my love for the eternal being. Through faith I don't renounce anything, on the contrary in faith I receive everything, exactly in the way it is said what one whose faith is like a mustard seed can move mountains. It takes a purely human courage to renounce the whole of temporality in order to win eternity, but I do indeed win it and cannot in all eternity renounce that, for that would be a self-contradiction; but it takes a paradoxical and humble courage then to grasp the whole of temporality on the strength of the absurd, and that courage is the courage of faith. Through faith Abraham did not renounce his claim on Isaac, through his faith he received Isaac. That rich young man, by virtue of his resignation, should have given everything away, but once he had done so the knight of faith would have to say to him: 'On the strength of the absurd you shall get every penny back, believe that!' And these words should by no means be a matter of indifference to the once rich young man; for if he gave his possessions away because he was bored with them, then his resignation was in a sorry state.

Temporality, finitude is what it all turns on. I am able by my own strength to renounce everything, and then find peace and repose in the pain; I can put up with everything even if that demon, more horrifying than the skull and bones that put terror into men's hearts — even if madness itself were to hold up the fool's costume before my eyes and I could tell from its look that it was I who was to put it on; I can still save my soul so long as it is more important for me that my love of God should triumph in me than my worldly happiness. A man can still, in that last moment, concentrate his whole soul in a single glance towards the heaven from which all good gifts come, and this glance is something both he and the one he seeks understand; it means he has nevertheless remained true to his love. Then he will calmly put on the costume. He who lacks this romanticism has sold his soul, whether he received a kingdom for it or a paltry piece of silver. But by my own strength I cannot get the least little thing of what belongs to finitude; for I am continually using my energy to renounce everything. By my own strength I can give up the princess, and I shall be no sulker but find joy and peace and repose in my pain, but with my own strength I cannot get her back again, for all that strength is precisely what I use to renounce my claim on her. But by faith, says that marvellous knight, by faith you will get her on the strength of the absurd.

Alas, this movement is one I cannot make! As soon as I want to begin it everything turns around and I flee back to the pain of resignation. I can swim in life, but for this mysterious floating I am too heavy. To exist in such a way that my opposition to existence expresses itself every instant as the most beautiful and safest harmony, that I cannot. And yet it must be glorious to get the princess, I say so every instant and the knight of resignation who doesn't say it is a deceiver, he has not had just one desire and he has not kept his desire young in its pain. Some might find it convenient enough that the desire is no longer alive, that the smart of pain has dulled; but such people are no knights. A free-born soul who caught himself at this would despise himself and make a fresh start, and above all not allow himself to be deceived in his soul. And yet it must be wonderful to get the princess, and yet it is only the knight of faith who is happy, only he is heir apparent to the finite, whereas the knight of resignation is a stranger, a foreigner. To get the princess in this way, to live in joy and happiness, in her company day in and day out – we have to allow, of course, that the knight of resignation, too, may get the princess, even though he has clearly perceived the impossibility of their future happiness – thus to live joyfully and happily in this way every moment on the strength of the absurd, every moment to see the sword hanging over the loved one's head and yet find, not repose in the pain of resignation, but joy on the strength of the absurd – that is wonderful. The one who does that, he is great, the only great one, the thought of it stirs my soul, which was never sparing in its admiration of greatness.

Now if everyone in my generation unwilling to stop at faith is really someone who has understood life's horror, has grasped Daub's meaning when he says that a soldier standing guard alone with a loaded gun by a powder magazine on a stormy night gets strange thoughts; if all those unwilling to stop at faith really are people who possess the strength of soul to grasp, and give themselves time to be alone with, the thought that what they wished was impossible, if all who are unwilling to stop at faith have really reconciled themselves in pain and been reconciled by pain; if all those unwilling to stop at faith have in addition (and unless they have done all this other they need not trouble themselves in matters of faith) performed that marvel, grasped the whole of existence on the strength of the absurd – then what I am writing is a speech in the highest praise of my generation by the least in it, by the one who could only make the movement of resignation. But why will they not *stop* at faith, why do we sometimes hear of people blushing to admit they have faith? That I cannot grasp. Should I ever come so far as to manage this movement, I'd drive thereafter with a coach-and-four.

Is it really the case, can all the *bourgeois* philistinism I see in life, and which I allow only my deeds and not my words to condemn, really be not what it seems? Is it really this marvel? That is certainly conceivable, for our hero of faith did indeed bear a striking resemblance to it, for our hero of faith was not even an ironist and humorist but something still higher. A lot is said in our time about irony and humour, particularly by people who have never succeeded in practising them but who nevertheless know how to explain everything. I am not altogether unfamiliar with these two passions, I know a little more about them than is to be found in German and German-Danish compendia. Therefore I know that these two passions differ essentially from the passion of faith. Irony and humour reflect also upon themselves and so belong in the sphere of infinite resignation, they owe their resilience to the individual's incommensurability with reality.

The last movement, the paradoxical movement of faith I cannot perform, be it a duty or whatever – though in fact I would be most willing to do it. Whether anyone has the right to say this must be up to him; it is a matter between him and the eternal being who is the object of faith whether he can reach an amicable agreement in this respect. What everyone can do, on the other hand, is perform the infinite movement of resignation, and I for my part would not think twice about pronouncing anyone a coward who thinks he can't. With faith it is another matter. But what no one has the right to do is let others suppose that faith is something inferior or that it is an easy matter, when in fact it is the greatest and most difficult of all.

Some understand the story of Abraham in another way. They praise God's mercy for giving him Isaac once again, the whole thing was just a trial. A trial – that can say a lot or little, yet the whole thing is as quickly done with as said. One mounts a winged horse, that very instant one is on the mountain in Moriah, the same instant one sees the ram. One forgets that Abraham rode on an ass, which can keep up no more than a leisurely pace, that he had a three-day journey, that he needed time to chop the firewood, bind Isaac, and sharpen the knife.

And yet one praises Abraham! The speaker might just as well sleep until fifteen minutes before speaking, his hearer might just as well sleep throughout the speech, since it all goes so smoothly, without trouble from either side. Should someone present be suffering from insomnia, that person might go home, sit down in a corner, and think: 'It's all over in a second, if you'll just wait a minute you'll see the ram and the trial is over.' Were the speaker to meet him in that state then I imagine he would advance on him in all his dignity and say: 'Wretch, that you can let your soul sink into such folly; there is no miracle, and all life is a trial.' The more effusive the speaker became the more heated he would grow and the better pleased with himself, and while he had noticed no congestion of the blood when speaking about Abraham, he could now feel the vein swelling on his forehead. He might perhaps be struck dumb were the sinner, calmly and with dignity, to reply: 'But that's what you preached last Sunday.'

So let us either forget all about Abraham or learn how to be horrified at the monstrous paradox which is the significance of his life, so that we can understand that our time like any other can be glad if it has faith. If Abraham is not a nonentity, a ghost, a piece of pomp one uses to pass time away, the mistake can never lie in the sinner's wanting to do like him; rather it is a question of seeing the greatness of Abraham's deed, so that the person may judge for himself whether he has the inclination and courage to be tried in such a thing. The comic contradiction in the speaker's behaviour was that he made Abraham into something insignificant and yet would forbid the other from carrying on in the same manner.

Should one perhaps not dare to speak about Abraham? I think one should. If I myself were to talk about him I would first depict the pain of the trial. For that I would suck all the fear, distress, and torment out of the father's suffering, like a leech, in order to be able to describe all that Abraham suffered while still believing. I would remind people that the journey lasted three days and well into the fourth; yes, those three-and-a-half days should be infinitely longer than the two thousand years separating me from Abraham. Then I would remind them that everyone, as I believe, should feel able to change their mind before beginning on such a thing, that it is possible at every moment to retract and turn back. If one does this I see no danger; nor am I afraid of arousing a desire in people to be put to the test like Abraham. But if one wants to market a cut-price version of Abraham and then still admonish people not to do what Abraham did, then that's just laughable.

What I intend now is to extract from the story of Abraham its dialectical element, in the form of *problemata*, in order to see how monstrous a paradox faith is, a paradox capable of making a murder into a holy act well pleasing to God, a paradox which gives Isaac back to Abraham, which no thought can grasp because faith begins precisely where thinking leaves off.

Problema I

Is There a Teleological Suspension of the Ethical?

The ethical as such is the universal, and as the universal it applies to everyone, which can be put from another point of view by saying that it applies at every moment. It rests immanently in itself, has nothing outside itself that is its *telos* [end, purpose] but is itself the *telos* for everything outside, and when that is taken up into it, it has no further to go. Seen as an immediate, no more than sensate and psychic, being, the single individual is the particular that has its *telos* in the universal, and the individual's ethical task is always to express himself in this, to abrogate his particularity so as to become the universal. As soon as the single individual wants to assert himself in his particularity, in direct opposition to the universal, he sins, and only by recognizing this can he again reconcile himself with the universal. Whenever, having entered the universal, the single individual feels an urge to assert his particularity, he is in a state of temptation, from which he can extricate himself only by surrendering his particularity to the universal in repentance. If that is the highest that can be said of man and his existence, then the ethical and a person's eternal blessedness, which is his *telos* in all eternity and at every moment, are identical; for in that case it would be a contradiction to say that one surrendered that *telos* (i.e. suspended it *teleologically*) since by suspending the *telos* one would be forfeiting it, while what is said to be suspended in this sense is not forfeited but preserved in something higher, the latter being precisely its *telos*.

If that is the case, then Hegel is right in his 'Good and Conscience' where he discusses man seen merely as the single individual and regards this way of seeing him as a 'moral form of evil' to be annulled in the teleology of the ethical life, so that the individual who stays at this stage is either in sin or in a state of temptation. Where Hegel goes wrong, on the other hand, is in talking about faith, in not protesting loudly and clearly against the honour and glory enjoyed by Abraham as the father of faith when he should really be remitted to some lower court for trial and exposed as a murderer.

For faith is just this paradox, that the single individual is higher than the universal, though in such a way, be it noted, that the movement is repeated, that is, that, having been in the universal, the single individual now sets himself apart as the particular above the universal. If that is not faith, then Abraham is done for and faith has never existed in the world, just because it has always existed. For if the ethical life is the highest and nothing incommensurable is left over in man, except in the sense of what is evil, i.e. the single individual who is to be expressed in the universal, then one needs no other categories than those of the Greek philosophers, or whatever can be logically deduced from them. This is something Hegel, who has after all made some study of the Greeks, ought not to have kept quiet about.

One not infrequently hears people who prefer to lose themselves in clichés rather than studies say that light shines over the Christian world, while paganism is shrouded in darkness. This kind of talk has always struck me as strange, since any reasonably deep thinker, any reasonably serious artist will still seek rejuvenation in the eternal youth of the Greeks. The explanation may be that they know not what to say, only that they have to say something. There is nothing wrong with saying that paganism did not have faith, but if this is to mean anything one must be a little clearer what one means by faith, otherwise one falls back into those clichés. It is easy to explain the whole of existence, faith included, and he is not the worst reckoner in life who counts on being admired for having such an explanation: for it is as Boileau says: '*un sot trouve toujours un plus sot, qui l'admire*' ['a fool can always find a greater fool who admires him'].

Faith is just this paradox, that the single individual as the particular is higher than the universal, is justified before the latter, not as subordinate but superior, though in such a way, be it noted, that it is the single individual who, having been subordinate to the universal as the particular, now by means of the universal becomes that individual who, as the particular, stands in an absolute relation to the absolute. This position cannot be mediated, for all mediation occurs precisely by virtue of the universal; it is and remains in all eternity a paradox, inaccessible to thought. And yet faith *is* this paradox. Or else (these are implications which I would ask the reader always to bear in mind, though it would be too complicated for me to spell them out each time) – or else faith has never existed just because it has always existed. And Abraham is done for.

That the individual can easily take this paradox for a temptation is true enough. But one should not keep it quiet on that account. True enough, too, that many people may have a natural aversion to the paradox, but that is no reason for making faith into something else so that they too can have it; while those who do have faith should be prepared to offer some criterion for distinguishing the paradox from a temptation.

Now the story of Abraham contains just such a teleological suspension of the ethical. There has been no want of sharp intellects and sound scholars who have found analogies to it. Their wisdom amounts to the splendid principle that basically everything is the same. If one looks a little closer I doubt very much whether one will find in the whole world a single analogy, except a later one that proves nothing, for the fact remains that Abraham represents faith, and that faith finds its proper expression in him whose life is not only the most paradoxical conceivable, but so paradoxical that it simply cannot be thought. He acts on the strength of the absurd; for it is precisely the absurd that as the single individual he is higher than the universal. This paradox cannot be mediated; for as soon as he tries Abraham will have to admit that he is in a state of temptation, and in that case he will never sacrifice Isaac, or if he has done so he must return repentantly to the universal. On the strength of the absurd he got Isaac back. Abraham is therefore at no instant the tragic hero, but something quite different, either a murderer or a man of faith. The middle-term that saves the tragic hero is something Abraham lacks. That is why I can understand a tragic hero, but not Abraham, even though in a certain lunatic sense I admire him more than all others.

Abraham's relation to Isaac, ethically speaking, is quite simply this, that the father should love the son more than himself. Yet within its own compass the ethical has several rankings; let us see whether this story contains any such higher expression of the ethical which might explain his behaviour ethically, justify him ethically for suspending the ethical duty to the son, yet without thereby exceeding the ethical's own teleology.

When an enterprise involving a whole nation is prevented, when such an enterprise is brought to a halt by heaven's disfavour, when divine wrath sends a dead calm which mocks every effort, when the soothsayer performs his sad task and proclaims that the deity demands a young girl as a sacrifice – then it is with heroism that the father has to make that sacrifice. Nobly will he hide his grief though he could wish he were 'the lowly man who dares to weep' and not the king who must bear himself as befits a king. And however solitarily the pain enters his breast, for he has only three confidants among his people, soon the entire population will be privy to his pain, but also to his deed, to the fact that for the well-being of the whole he was willing to offer that girl, his daughter, this lovely young maiden. Oh, what bosom! What fair cheeks! What flaxen hair! And the daughter will touch him with her tears, and the father avert his face, but the hero will raise the knife. And when the news of this reaches the ancestral home all the beauteous maidens of Greece will blush with animation, and were the daughter a bride the betrothed would not be angered but proud to have been party to the father's deed, because the maiden belonged to him more tenderly than to the father.

When that bold judge, who saved Israel in the hour of need binds God and himself in one breath with the same promise, then it is with heroism that he is to transform the young girl's jubilation, the beloved daughter's joy, to sorrow, and all Israel will grieve with her maidenly youth; but every free-born man will understand Jephthah, every stout-hearted woman admire him, and every maiden in Israel will want to do as his daughter; for what good would it be for Jephthah to triumph by making his promise but fail to keep it? Would the victory not be taken once more from the people?

When a son forgets his duty, when the State entrusts the father with the sword of judgement, when the laws demand punishment at the father's hand, then it is with heroism that the father must forget that the guilty one is his son. Nobly will he hide his pain, but in the nation there will be not one, not even the son, who fails to admire the father, and every time the laws of Rome are interpreted it will be recalled that many interpreted them more learnedly but none more gloriously than Brutus.

On the other hand, if it had been while his fleet was being borne by wind under full sail to its destination that Agamemnon had sent that messenger who brought Iphigenia to the sacrifice; if unbound by any promise that would decide the fate of his people Jephthah had said to his daughter: 'Sorrow now for two months henceforth over the short day of your youth, for I shall sacrifice you'; if Brutus had had a righteous son and still called upon the lictors to execute him – who would understand them? If to the question, why did you do it?, these three had replied: 'It is a trial in which we are being tested', would one then have understood them better?

When at the decisive moment Agamemnon, Jephthah, and Brutus heroically overcome their pain, have heroically given up the loved one, and have only the outward deed to perform, then never a noble soul in the world will there be but sheds tears of sympathy for their pain, tears of admiration for their deed. But if at that decisive moment these three men had added to the heroism with which they bore their pain the little words 'It won't happen', who then would understand them? If in explanation they added: 'We believe it on the strength of the absurd', who then would understand them better? For who would not readily understand that it was absurd? But who would understand that for that reason one could believe it?

The difference between the tragic hero and Abraham is obvious enough. The tragic hero stays within the ethical. He lets an expression of the ethical have its *telos* in a higher expression of the ethical; he reduces the ethical relation between father and son, or daughter and father, to a sentiment that has its dialectic in its relation to the idea of the ethical life. Here, then, there can be no question of a teleological suspension of the ethical itself.

With Abraham it is different. In his action he overstepped the ethical altogether, and had a higher *telos* outside it, in relation to which he suspended it. For how could one ever bring Abraham's action into relationship with the universal? How could any point of contact ever be discovered between what Abraham did and the universal other than that Abraham overstepped it? It is not to save a nation, not to uphold the idea of the State, that Abraham did it, not to appease angry gods. If there was any question of the deity's being angry, it could only have been Abraham he was angry with, and Abraham's whole action stands in no relation to the universal, it is a purely private undertaking. While, then, the tragic hero is great through his deed's being an expression of the ethical life, Abraham is great through an act of purely personal virtue. There is no higher expression of the ethical in Abraham's life than that the father shall love the son. The ethical in the sense of the ethical life is quite out of the question. In so far as the universal was there at all it was latent in Isaac, concealed as it were in his loins, and it would have to cry out with Isaac's mouth: 'Don't do it, you are destroying everything.'

Then why does Abraham do it? For God's sake, and what is exactly the same, for his own. He does it for the sake of God because God demands this proof of his faith; he does it for his own sake in order to be able to produce the proof. The unity here is quite properly expressed in the saying in which this relationship has always been described: it is a trial, a temptation. A temptation, but what does that mean? What we usually call a temptation is something that keeps a person from carrying out a duty, but here the temptation is the ethical itself which would keep him from doing God's will. But then what is the duty? For the duty is precisely the expression of God's will.

Here we see the need for a new category for understanding Abraham. Such a relationship to the divine is unknown to paganism. The tragic hero enters into no private relationship with God, but the ethical is the divine and therefore the paradox in the divine can be mediated in the universal.

Abraham cannot be mediated, which can also be put by saying he cannot speak. The moment I speak I express the universal, and when I do not no one can understand me. So the moment Abraham wants to express himself in the universal, he has to say that his situation is one of temptation, for he has no higher expression of the universal that overrides the universal he transgresses.

Thus while Abraham arouses my admiration, he also appals me. The person who denies himself and sacrifices himself for duty gives up the finite in order to grasp on to the infinite; he is secure enough. The tragic hero gives up what is certain for what is still more certain, and the eye of the beholder rests confidently upon him. But the person who gives up the universal to grasp something still higher that is not the universal, what does he do? Can this be anything but temptation? And if it were something else but the individual were mistaken, what salvation is there for him? He suffers all the pain of the tragic hero, he brings all his joy in the world to nothing, he abandons everything, and perhaps the same instant debars himself from that exalted joy so precious to him that he would buy it at any price. That person the beholder cannot at all understand, nor let his eye rest upon him with confidence. Perhaps what the believer intends just cannot be done, after all it is unthinkable. Or if it could be done and the individual had misunderstood the deity, what salvation would there be for him? The tragic hero, he needs tears and he claims them; yes, where was that envious eye so barren as not to weep with Agamemnon, but where was he whose soul was so confused as to presume to weep for Abraham? The tragic hero has done with his deed at a definite moment in time, but in the course of time he achieves something no less important, he seeks out the one whose soul is beset with sorrow, whose breast cannot draw air for its stifled sighs, whose thoughts, weighed down with tears, hang heavy upon him; he appears before him, he breaks the spell of grief, loosens the corset, coaxes forth the tear by making the sufferer forget his own suffering in his. Abraham one cannot weep over. One approaches him with a *horror religiosus* [holy terror] like that in which Israel approached Mount Sinai. What if the lonely man who climbs the mountain in Moriah, whose peak soars heaven-high over the plains of Aulis, is not a sleepwalker who treads surefootedly over the abyss, while someone standing at the foot of the mountain, seeing him there, trembles with anxiety and out of respect and fear dares not even shout to him – what if he should be distracted, what if he has made a mistake? – Thanks! And thanks again, to whoever holds out to one who has been assaulted and left naked by life's sorrows, holds out to him the leaf of the word with which to hide his misery. Thanks to you, great Shakespeare!, you who can say everything, everything, everything exactly as it is – and yet why was this torment one you never gave voice to? Was it perhaps that you kept it to yourself, like the beloved whose name one still cannot bear the world to mention? For a poet buys this power of words to utter all the grim secrets of others at the cost of a little secret he himself cannot utter, and a poet is not an apostle, he casts devils out only by the power of the devil.

But now when the ethical is thus teleologically suspended, how does the single individual in whom it is suspended exist? He exists as the particular in opposition to the universal. Does this mean he sins? For this is the form of sin looked at ideally, just as the fact that the child does not sin because it is not conscious of its own existence as such does not mean that, looked at ideally, its existence is not that of sin or that the ethical does not make its demands of the child at every moment. If this form cannot be said to repeat itself in a way other than that of sin, then judgement has been delivered upon Abraham. Then how did Abraham exist? He had faith. That is the paradox that keeps him at the extremity and which he cannot make clear to anyone else, for the paradox is that he puts himself as the single individual in an absolute relation to the absolute. Is he justified? His justification is, once again, the paradox; for if he is the paradox it is not by virtue of being anything universal, but of being the particular.

How does the single individual assure himself that he is justified? It is a simple enough matter to level the whole of existence down to the idea of the State or to a concept of society. If one does that one can no doubt also mediate; for in this way one does not come to the paradox at all, to the single individual's as such being higher than the universal, which I can also put pointedly in a proposition of Pythagoras's, that the odd numbers are more perfect than the even. Should one happen to catch word of an answer in the direction of the paradox in our time, it will no doubt go like this: 'That's to be judged by the outcome.' A hero who has become the scandal of his generation, aware that he is a paradox that cannot be understood, cries undaunted to his contemporaries: 'The future will show I was right!' This cry is heard less frequently nowadays, for as our age to its detriment produces no heroes, so it has the advantage that it also produces few caricatures. Whenever nowadays we hear the words 'That's to be judged by the outcome' we know immediately with whom we have the honour of conversing. Those who speak thus are a populous tribe which, to give them a common name, I shall call the 'lecturers'. They live in their thoughts, secure in life, they have a *permanent* position and *sure* prospects in a well-organized State; they are separated by centuries, even millennia, from the convulsions of existence; they have no fear that such things could happen again; what would the police and the newspapers say? Their lifework is to judge the great, to judge them according to the outcome. Such conduct in respect of greatness betrays a strange mixture of arrogance and pitifulness, arrogance because they feel called to pass judgement, pitifulness because they feel their lives unrelated in even the remotest manner to those of the great. Surely anyone with a speck of *erectior ingenii* [nobility of mind] cannot

73

become so completely the cold and clammy mollusc as to lose sight altogether, in approaching the great, of the fact that ever since the Creation it has been accepted practice for the outcome to come last, and that if one is really to learn something from the great it is precisely the beginning one must attend to. If anyone on the verge of action should judge himself according to the outcome, he would never begin. Even though the result may gladden the whole world, that cannot help the hero; for he knows the result only when the whole thing is over, and that is not how he becomes a hero, but by virtue of the fact that he began.

But in any case the outcome in its dialectic (in so far as it is finitude's answer to the infinite question) is totally incompatible with the existence of the hero. Or are we to take it that Abraham was justified in relating himself as the single individual to the universal by the fact that he got Isaac by a *marvel*? Had Abraham actually sacrificed Isaac, would that have meant he was less justified?

But it is the outcome that arouses our curiosity, as with the conclusion of a book; one wants nothing of the fear, the distress, the paradox. One flirts with the outcome aesthetically; it comes as unexpectedly and yet as effortlessly as a prize in the lottery; and having heard the outcome one is improved. And yet no robber of temples hard-labouring in chains is so base a criminal as he who plunders the holy in this way, and not even Judas, who sold his master for thirty pieces of silver, is more contemptible than the person who would thus offer greatness for sale.

It goes against my nature to speak inhumanly of

greatness, to let its grandeur fade into an indistinct out-
line at an immense distance, or represent it as great
without the human element in it coming to the fore –
whence it ceases to be the great; for it is not what
happens to me that makes me great, but what I do, and
there is surely no one who thinks that anyone became
great by winning the big lottery prize. Even of a person
born in humble circumstances I ask that he should not
be so inhuman towards himself as to be unable to think
of the king's castle except at a distance and by dreaming
of its grandeur indistinctly, wanting to exalt it and simultaneously destroying its grandeur by exalting it in such
a debasing way. I ask that he be human enough to
approach and bear himself with confidence and dignity
there too. He should not be so inhuman as shamelessly
to want to violate every rule of respect by storming into
the king's salon straight from the street – he loses more
by doing that than the king; on the contrary he should
find pleasure in observing every rule of decorum with a
glad and confident enthusiasm, which is just what will
make him frank and open-hearted. This is only an analogy, for the difference here is only a very imperfect
expression of the spiritual distance. I ask everyone not
to think so inhumanly of himself as to dare not set foot
in those palaces where not just the memory of the chosen
lives on but the chosen themselves. He should not push
himself shamelessly forward and thrust upon them his
kinship with them, he should feel happy every time he
bows before them, but be frank and confident and always
something more than a cleaning woman; for unless he
wants to be more than that he will never come in there.

And what will help him are exactly the fear and distress in which the great are tried, for otherwise, at least if there is a drop of red blood in him, they will merely arouse his righteous envy. And whatever can only be great at a distance, whatever people want to exalt with empty and hollow phrases, that they themselves reduce to nothing.

Was there ever in the world anyone as great as that blessed woman, the mother of God, the Virgin Mary? And yet how do people speak of her? To say she was favoured among women doesn't make her great, and if it were not for the odd fact that those who listen can think as inhumanly as those who speak, surely every young girl would ask, why am I not favoured too? And had I nothing more to say I should by no means dismiss such a question as stupid; for as regards favours, abstractly considered, everyone is equally entitled. What is left out is the distress, the fear, the paradox. My thought is as pure as the next man's and surely the thought of anyone able to think in this way will be pure; if not, something dreadful is in store; for a person who has once called these images to mind cannot be rid of them again, and if he sins against them, then in their quiet wrath, more terrifying than the clamour of ten voracious critics, they will wreak their awful vengeance on him. No doubt Mary bore the child miraculously, but it went with Mary 'after the manner of women', and such a time is one of fear, distress, and paradox. No doubt the angel was a ministering spirit, but he was not an obliging one who went round to all the other young girls in Israel and said:

'Do not despise Mary, something out of the ordinary is happening to her.' The angel came only to Mary, and no one could understand her. Yet what woman was done greater indignity than Mary, and isn't it true here too that those whom God blesses he damns in the same breath? This is the spirit's understanding of Mary, and she is not at all – as it offends me to say, though even more so that people have mindlessly and irresponsibly thought of her thus – she is not at all the fine lady sitting in her finery and playing with a divine child. Yet for saying notwithstanding, 'Behold the handmaid of the Lord', she is great, and it seems to me that it should not be difficult to explain why she became the mother of God. She needs no worldly admiration, as little as Abraham needs our tears, for she was no heroine and he no hero, but both of them became greater than that, not by any means by being relieved of the distress, the agony, and the paradox, but because of these.

Great indeed it is when the poet presents his tragic hero for popular admiration and dares to say: 'Weep for him, for he deserves it'; for there is greatness in meriting the tears of those who deserve to shed them; great indeed for the poet to dare hold the crowd in check, dare discipline people into testing their own worthiness to weep for the hero, for the waste-water of snivellers is a degradation of the holy. But greater than all these is that the knight of faith dares to say even to the noble person who would weep for him: 'Do not weep for me, but weep for yourself.'

One is stirred, one harks back to those beautiful times,

sweet tender longings lead one to the goal of one's desire, to see Christ walking about in the promised land. One forgets the fear, the distress, the paradox. Was it so easy a matter not to be mistaken? Was it not a fearful thought that this man who walked among the others was God? Was it not terrifying to sit down to eat with him? Was it so easy a matter to become an apostle? But the outcome, eighteen centuries, that helps; it helps that shabby deception wherein one deceives oneself and others. I do not feel brave enough to wish to be contemporary with such events, but for that reason I do not judge harshly of those who were mistaken, nor think meanly of those who saw the truth.

But now I return to Abraham. In the time before the outcome either Abraham was a murderer every minute or we stay with the paradox which is higher than all mediation.

So Abraham's story contains a teleological suspension of the ethical. He has, as the single individual, become higher than the universal. This is the paradox which cannot be mediated. How he got into it is just as inexplicable as how he stayed in it. If this is not how it is with Abraham, then he is not even a tragic hero but a murderer. To want to go on calling him the father of faith, to talk of this to those who are only concerned with words, is thoughtless. A tragic hero can become a human being by his own strength, but not the knight of faith. When a person sets out on the tragic hero's admittedly hard path there are many who could lend him advice; but he who walks the narrow path of faith no one can advise, no one understand. Faith is a marvel, and yet no human being is excluded from it; for that in which all human life is united is passion,* and faith is a passion.

---

* Lessing has somewhere made similar remarks from a purely aes-thetic point of view. In the passage in question he actually wants to show that sorrow too can express itself with wit. To that end he quotes the words spoken on a particular occasion by the unfortunate English king, Edward II. As contrast he quotes from Diderot: a story of a farmer's wife and a remark of hers, and then continues: 'That too was wit, and the wit of a peasant at that: but the situation made it inevitable. Consequently one mustn't try to find the excuse for the witty expression of pain and of sorrow in the fact that the person who uttered them was superior, well-educated, intelligent, and witty as well, *for the passions make all men again equal* . . . the explanation lies in the fact that in the same situation probably everyone would have said the same thing. The peasant woman's thought is one a queen might just as well have had, just as what the king said on that occasion could, and no doubt would, have been said by a peasant.'

Problema II

Is There an Absolute Duty to God?

The ethical is the universal and as such, in turn, the divine. It is therefore correct to say that all duty is ultimately duty to God; but if one cannot say more one says in effect that really I have no duty to God. The duty becomes duty to God by being referred to God, but I do not enter into relation with God in the duty itself. Thus it is a duty to love one's neighbour; it is a duty in so far as it is referred to God; yet it is not God that I come in relation to in the duty but the neighbour I love. If, in this connection, I then say that it is my duty to love God, I in fact only utter a tautology, in so far as 'God' is understood in an altogether abstract sense as the divine: i.e. the universal, i.e. duty. The whole of human existence is in that case entirely self-enclosed, as a sphere, and the ethical is at once the limit and completion. God becomes an invisible, vanishing point, an impotent thought, and his power is to be found only in the ethical, which fills all existence. So if it should occur to someone to want to love God in some other sense than that mentioned, he is merely being extravagant and loves a phantom which, if it only had the strength to speak, would say to him: 'Stay where you belong, I don't ask for your love.' If it should occur to someone to want to love God in another way, this love would be suspect, like the love referred to by Rousseau when he talks of a person's loving the Kaffirs instead of his neighbour.

Now if all this is correct, if there is nothing incommensurable in a human life, but any incommensurability were due only to some chance from which nothing followed so far as existence is looked at in light of the Idea, then Hegel would be right. But where he is wrong is in talking about faith or in letting Abraham be looked on as its father; for in this latter he has passed sentence both on Abraham and on faith. In the Hegelian philosophy *das Äussere (die Entäusserung)* [the outer, the externalization] is higher than *das Innere* [the inner]. This is often illustrated by an example. The child is *das Innere*, the man *das Äussere*; which is why the child is determined precisely by the outer, and conversely the man as *das Äussere* by the inner. Faith, on the contrary, is this paradox, that interiority is higher than exteriority, or to recall again an expression we used above, that the odd number is higher than the even.

In the ethical view of life, then, it is the individual's task to divest himself of the determinant of interiority and give it an expression in the exterior. Whenever the individual shrinks from doing so, whenever he wants to stay inside, or slip back into, the inner determinant of feeling, mood, etc., he commits an offence, he is in a state of temptation. The paradox of faith is this, that there is an interiority that is incommensurable with the exterior, an interiority which, it should be stressed, is not identical with the first [that of the child], but is a new interiority. This must not be overlooked. Recent philosophy has allowed itself without further ado to substitute the immediate for 'faith'. If one does that it is ridiculous to deny that faith has existed through all ages. Faith in such a case keeps fairly ordinary company, it belongs with feeling, mood, idiosyncrasy, hysteria and the rest. So far philosophy is right to say one should not stop at that. But there is nothing to warrant philosophy's speaking in this manner. Prior to faith there is a movement of infinity, and only then enters faith, *nec opinate* [unexpectedly], on the strength of the absurd. This I am very well able to understand, without claiming thereby to have faith. If faith is no more than what philosophy passes it off as then Socrates himself already went further, much further, rather than the converse, that he didn't come that far. He made the movement of infinity intellectually. His ignorance is the infinite resignation. That task is in itself a match for human strength, even if people nowadays scorn it; yet it is only when this has been done, only when the individual has exhausted himself in the infinite, that he reaches the point where faith can emerge.

Then faith's paradox is this, that the single individual is higher than the universal, that the single individual (to recall a theological distinction less in vogue these days) determines his relation to the universal through his relation to the absolute, not his relation to the absolute through his relation to the universal. The paradox can also be put by saying that there is an absolute duty to God; for in this tie of obligation the individual relates himself absolutely, as the single individual, to the absolute. When people now say that it is a duty to love God, it is in a sense quite different from the above; for if this duty is absolute the ethical is reduced to the relative. It doesn't follow, nevertheless, that [the ethical] is to be done away with. Only that it gets a quite different expression, the paradoxical expression, so that, e.g., love of God can cause the knight of faith to give his love of his neighbour the opposite expression to that which is his duty ethically speaking.

Unless this is how it is, faith has no place in existence; and faith is then a temptation, and Abraham is done for, since he gave in to it.

This paradox does not allow of mediation: for it rests precisely on the single individual's being only the single individual. As soon as this individual wants to express his absolute duty in the universal, becomes conscious of it in the latter, he knows he is in a state of temptation, and then, even if he otherwise resists the temptation, he does not come to fulfil that so-called absolute duty, and if he does not resist it he sins even if *realiter* [independently of his inclination, wishes, state of mind] his act is the one that was his absolute duty. Thus what could Abraham have done? If he had wanted to say to someone: 'I love Isaac more than everything in the world, and that's why it is so hard for me to sacrifice him', the person would surely have shaken his head and said: 'Then why sacrifice him?', or if he was a perceptive fellow perhaps he might even have seen through Abraham, realized that he was betraying feelings which stood in flagrant contradiction with his deed.

In the story of Abraham we find just such a paradox. Ethically speaking his relation to Isaac is this, that the father is to love the son. This ethical relationship is reduced to the relative as against the absolute relation to God. To the question, why?, Abraham has no other answer than that it is a trial and a temptation, which, as remarked above, is what makes it a unity of being for both God's sake and his own. These two are also correlative in ordinary usage. Thus when we see someone do something that doesn't conform with the universal, we say, 'He can hardly be doing that for the sake of God', meaning by this that he did it for his own sake. The paradox of faith has lost the intermediate term, i.e. the universal. On the one hand it contains the expression of extreme egoism (doing this dreadful deed for his own sake) and on the other the expression of the most absolute devotion (doing it for God's sake). Faith itself cannot be mediated into the universal, for in that case it would be cancelled. Faith is this paradox, and the single individual is quite unable to make himself intelligible to anyone. One might suppose the single individual could make himself understood to another individual who is in the same situation. Such a view would be unthinkable were it not that nowadays people try in so many ways to sneak their way into greatness. The one knight of faith simply cannot help the other. Either the single individual becomes a knight of faith himself by putting on the paradox, or he never becomes one. Partnership in these regions is quite unthinkable. If there is any more precise explanation of the idea behind the sacrifice of Isaac, it is one that the individual can only give to himself. And supposing one could settle, even with some exactitude, in universal terms, how to understand the case of Isaac (which would in any case be the most absurd self-contradiction, namely that the single individual who stands precisely outside the universal be brought in under universal categories, when he is expressly to act as the single individual outside the universal), the individual could still never be assured of [the truth of] this explanation by others, but only by himself as the single individual. So even if someone were so cowardly and base as to want to be a knight of faith on someone else's responsibility, he would never become one; for only the single individual becomes one, as the single individual, and this is the knight's greatness, as I can well understand without being party to it, since I lack courage; though also his terror, as I can understand even better.

As everyone knows, Luke 14.26 presents a remarkable teaching on the absolute duty to God: 'If any man come to me, and hate not his father, and mother, and wife, and children, and brethren, and sisters, yea, and his own life also, he cannot be my disciple.' This is a hard saying, who can bear to hear it? And for that reason it is heard very seldom. Yet this silence is only a futile evasion. The student of theology learns, however, that these words occur in the New Testament, and in one or another exegetical aid he finds the information that *misein* [to hate], both here and in some other passages, is used *per meiosin* [by adopting a weaker sense] to mean: *minus diligo* [love less], *posthabeo* [give less priority to], *non colo* [show no respect to], *nihil facio* [make nothing of]. The context in which these words occur seems, however, not to corroborate this tasteful explanation. For in the next verse [but one] there is a story about someone who plans to erect a tower but first makes some estimate of his capacity to do so, lest he be the object of ridicule later. The close link between this story and the verse quoted seems to suggest precisely that the words are to be taken in as terrifying a sense as possible in order that everyone should examine his own ability to erect the building.

If this pious and tender-minded exegete, who thinks he can smuggle Christianity into the world by haggling in this way, should succeed in convincing anyone that grammatically, linguistically, and *kata analogian* [by analogy] this was the meaning of the passage, then it is to be hoped that in so doing he also manages to convince the same person that Christianity is one of the most miserable things in the world. For the teaching which in one of its most lyrical outpourings, where the sense of its eternal validity swells up most strongly, has nothing to offer but a sounding phrase that signifies nothing and suggests only that one is to be less kind, less attentive, more indifferent; the teaching which, just as it seems to want to tell us something terrible, ends up in drivel rather than terror – that teaching is certainly not worth standing up for.

The words are terrible, but I feel sure they can be understood without the person who understands them necessarily having the courage to do as they say. And yet there must be honesty enough to admit what is there, to confess to its greatness even if one lacks the courage oneself. Anyone who manages that will not exclude himself from a share in the beautiful story, for in a way it contains a kind of comfort for the man who lacks courage to begin building the tower. But he must be honest and not pass off this lack of courage as humility, since on the contrary it is pride, while the courage of faith is the only humble courage.

One now sees readily that if the passage is to have any sense, it must be understood literally. It is God who demands absolute love. Anyone who, in demanding a person's love, thinks this must be proved by the latter's becoming lukewarm towards all that was hitherto dear to him, is not simply an egoist but a fool, and anyone demanding such a love would simultaneously sign his own death-warrant in so far as his life is bound up in this love he craves. A husband requires his wife to leave her father and mother, but were he to regard it as proof of her special love for him that for his sake she became a lukewarm, indolent daughter, etc., then he would be an idiot among idiots. Had he any notion of what love was, he would want to discover – and should he discover it see in this an assurance that his wife loved him more than any other in the kingdom – that she was perfect in her love as daughter and sister. So what would be considered a sign of egoism and stupidity in a person, one is supposed with the help of an exegete to regard as a worthy conception of the deity.

But how then *hate* them? I shall not take up the human love/hate distinction here, not because I have so much against it, since at least it is a passionate distinction, but it is egoistic and so does not fit here. If I regard the requirement as a paradox, on the other hand, then I understand it, i.e. understand it in the way one can understand a paradox. The absolute duty can then lead to what ethics would forbid, but it can by no means make the knight of faith have done with loving. This is shown by Abraham. The moment he is ready to sacrifice Isaac, the ethical expression for what he does is this: he hates Isaac. But if he actually hates Isaac he can be certain that God does not require this of him; for Cain and Abraham are not the same. Isaac he must love with all his soul. When God asks for Isaac, Abraham must if possible love him even more, and only then can he *sacrifice* him; for it is indeed this love of Isaac that in its paradoxical opposition to his love of God makes his act a sacrifice. But the distress and anguish in the paradox is that, humanly speaking, he is quite incapable of making himself understood. Only in the moment when his act is in absolute contradiction with his feeling, only then does he sacrifice Isaac, but the reality of his act is that in virtue of which he belongs to the universal, and there he is and remains a murderer.

Furthermore, the passage in Luke must be understood in such a way that one grasps that the knight of faith has no higher expression whatever of the universal (as the ethical) which can save him. Thus if we imagine the Church were to demand this sacrifice of one of its members, then all we have is a tragic hero. For qualitatively the idea of the Church is no different from that of the State, inasmuch as the individual can enter it by common mediation, and in so far as the individual has entered the paradox he does not arrive at the idea of the Church; he doesn't get out of the paradox either, but must find either his blessedness or his damnation inside it. An ecclesiastical hero expresses the universal in his deed, and no one in the Church, not even his father or mother, etc., will fail to understand him. But he is not the knight of faith, and has also a different answer from Abraham's; he doesn't say it is a trial or a temptation in which he is being tested.

One as a rule refrains from citing texts like the one in Luke. There is a fear of letting people loose, a fear that the worst will happen once the individual enjoys carrying on like an individual. Moreover living as the individual is thought to be the easiest thing of all, and it is the universal that people must be coerced into becoming. I can share neither this fear nor this opinion, and for the same reason. No person who has learned that to exist as the individual is the most terrifying thing of all will be afraid of saying it is the greatest. But then he mustn't say it in a way that makes his words a pitfall for somebody on the loose, but rather in a way that helps that person into the universal, even though his words can make some small allowance for greatness. The person who dares not mention such passages dares not mention Abraham either, and to think that existing as the individual is an easy enough matter implies a very dubious indirect admission with regard to oneself; for someone who really respects himself and is concerned for his own soul is assured of the fact that a person living under his own supervision in the world at large lives in greater austerity and seclusion than a maiden in her lady's bower. That there may be some who need coercion, who if given free rein would riot in selfish pleasure like unbridled beasts, is no doubt true, but one should show precisely by the fact that one knows how to speak with fear and trembling that one is not of their number. And out of respect for greatness one should indeed speak, lest it be forgotten for fear of the harm which surely won't arise if one speaks as one who knows it is the great, knows its terrors, and if one doesn't know these one doesn't know its greatness either.

Let us then consider more closely the distress and fear in the paradox of faith. The tragic hero renounces himself in order to express the universal; the knight of faith renounces the universal in order to be the particular. As mentioned, it all depends on how one is placed. Someone who believes it is a simple enough matter to be the individual can always be certain that he is not the knight of faith; for stragglers and vagrant geniuses are not men of faith. Faith's knight knows on the contrary that it is glorious to belong to the universal. He knows it is beautiful and benign to be the particular who translates himself into the universal, the one who so to speak makes a clear and elegant edition of himself, as immaculate as possible, and readable for all; he knows it is refreshing to become intelligible to oneself in the universal, so that he understands the universal and everyone who understands him understands the universal through him in turn, and both rejoice in the security of the universal. He knows it is beautiful to be born as the particular with the universal as his home, his friendly abode, which receives him straightaway with open arms when he wishes to stay there. But he also knows that higher up there winds a lonely path, narrow and steep; he knows it is terrible to be born in solitude outside the universal, to walk without meeting a single traveller. He knows very well where he is, and how he is related to men.

Humanly speaking he is insane and cannot make himself understood to anyone. And yet 'insane' is the mildest expression for him. If he isn't viewed thus, he is a hypocrite and the higher up the path he climbs, the more dreadful a hypocrite he becomes.

The knight of faith knows it gives inspiration to surrender oneself to the universal, that it takes courage to do so, but also that there is a certain security in it, just because it is for the universal; he knows it is glorious to be understood by every noble mind, and in such a way that even the beholder is thereby ennobled. This he knows and he feels as though bound, he could wish this was the task he had been set. Thus surely Abraham must have now and then wished that the task was to love Isaac in a way meet and fitting for a father, as all would understand and as would be remembered for all time; he must have wished his task was to sacrifice Isaac for the universal, so as to inspire fathers to illustrious deeds – and he must have been well nigh horrified by the thought that for him such wishes were merely temptations and must be treated as such; for he knew it was a solitary path he trod, and that he was doing nothing for the universal but only being tested and tried himself. Or what was it Abraham did for the universal? Let me speak humanly about it, really humanly! It takes him seventy years to get the son of his old age. What others get soon enough and have long joy of takes him seventy years. And why? Because he is being tested and tried. Is that not insanity? But Abraham believed, and only Sarah wavered and got him to take Hagar as his concubine –

but for that reason he also had to drive Hagar away. He gets Isaac and now he is to be tried once again. He knew it was glorious to express the universal, glorious to live with Isaac. But this is not the task. He knew it would have been a kingly deed to sacrifice such a son for the universal, he himself would have found repose in that, and everyone would have 'reposed' in their praise of his deed, just as the vowel 'reposes' in its quiescent letter; but this is not the task – he is being tried. That Roman general famous under the name of Cunctator halted the enemy by his delaying tactics, yet what kind of delayer is Abraham by comparison? But he isn't saving the State. This is the sum of one hundred and thirty years. Who can bear it? Should his contemporaries – if they can be called that – not say: 'There is an eternal procrastinating with Abraham; when he finally gets a son – and that took long enough – he wants to sacrifice him; he must be demented; and if only he could explain why he wanted to do that, but no, it's always a "trial"'? Nor could Abraham offer any further explanation, for his life is like a book put under divine seizure and which will never become *publici juris* [public property].

This is what is terrible. Anyone who doesn't see this can always be quite certain he is no knight of faith; but anyone who does see it will not deny that the step of even the most tried tragic hero goes like a dance compared with the slow and creeping progress of the knight of faith. And having seen it and realized he does not have the courage to understand it, he must at least have some idea of the wonderful glory achieved by that knight in becoming God's confidant, the Lord's friend, and – to speak really humanly – in addressing God in heaven as 'Thou', while even the tragic hero only addresses him in the third person.

The tragic hero is soon finished, his struggle is soon at an end; he makes the infinite movement and is now safe in the universal. But the knight of faith is kept awake, for he is under constant trial and can turn back in repentance to the universal at any moment, and this possibility can just as well be a temptation as the truth. Enlightenment as to which is something he can get from no one; otherwise he would be outside the paradox.

The knight of faith has therefore, first and foremost, the passion to concentrate the whole of the ethical that he violates in one single thing; he can be sure that he really loves Isaac with all his soul.* If he cannot be that, he is in

* I will explain once more the difference in the collision as between the tragic hero and the knight of faith. The tragic hero assures himself that the ethical obligation [to his son, daughter, etc.] is totally present in him by virtue of the fact that he transforms it into a wish. Thus Agamemnon can say: this is my proof that I am not violating my paternal obligation, that my duty [to Iphigenia] is my only wish. Here, then, wish and duty match one another. Happy my lot in life if my wish coincides with my duty, and conversely; and most people's task in life is exactly to stay under their obligation, and by their enthusiasm to transform it into their wish. The tragic hero renounces what he wishes in order to accomplish his duty. For the knight of faith, wish and duty are also identical, but the knight of faith is required to give up both. So when renouncing in resignation what he wishes he finds no repose; for it is after all his duty [that he is giving up]. If he stays under his obligation and keeps his wish he will not become the knight of faith; for the absolute duty requires precisely that he give up [the duty that is identical with the wish]. The tragic hero acquires a higher expression of duty, but not an absolute duty.

a state of temptation. Next, he has the passion to evoke this certainty intact in a twinkling and in as fully valid a way as in the first instance. If he cannot do this he doesn't get started, for then he must constantly start again from the beginning. The tragic hero, too, concentrates in one single thing the ethical that he teleologically violates, but in this thing he has resort to the universal. The knight of faith has only himself, and it is there the terrible lies. Most people let their ethical obligations last a day at a time, but then they never reach this passionate concentration, this energetic awareness. The tragic hero can in a sense be helped by the universal in acquiring these, but the knight of faith is alone about everything. The tragic hero acts and finds his point of rest in the universal, the knight of faith is kept in constant tension. Agamemnon gives up his claim to Iphigenia, thereby finds his point of rest in the universal, and now proceeds to give her in sacrifice. If Agamemnon had not made the movement, if in the decisive moment, instead of a passionate concentration, his soul had been lost in common chatter about his having several daughters, and *vielleicht das Ausserordentliche* [perhaps something extraordinary] could happen – then naturally he would not be a hero but a case for charity. Abraham has the hero's concentration too, even though in him it is much more difficult since he has no resort at all to the universal, but he makes one movement more through which he concentrates his soul back upon the marvel. If Abraham hadn't done that he would only have been an Agamemnon, provided it can be explained how his willingness to sacrifice Isaac can be justified other than by its benefiting the universal.

Whether the individual is now really in a state of temptation or a knight of faith, only the individual can decide. Still, it is possible on the basis of the paradox to construct certain criteria which even someone not in it can understand. The true knight of faith is always absolute isolation, the false knight is sectarian. The latter involves an attempt to leap off the narrow path of the paradox in order to become a tragic hero on the cheap. The tragic hero expresses the universal and sacrifices himself for it. The sectarian Master Jackel has instead his private theatre, [i.e.] several good friends and companions who represent the universal about as well as the public witnesses in *The Golden Snuffbox* represent justice. The knight of faith, on the other hand, is the paradox, he is the individual, absolutely nothing but the individual, without connections and complications. This is the terror that the puny sectarian cannot endure. Instead of learning from this that he is incapable of greatness and plainly admitting it, something I cannot but approve since it is what I myself do, the poor wretch thinks he will achieve it by joining company with other poor wretches. But it won't at all work, no cheating is tolerated in the world of spirit. A dozen sectarians link arms, they know nothing at all of the lonely temptations in store for the knight of faith and which he dare not shun just because it would be more terrible still were he presumptuously to force his way forward. The sectarians deafen each other with their clang and clatter, hold dread at bay with their shrieks, and a whooping Sunday-outing like this thinks it is storming heaven, believes it is following the same path as the knight of faith who, in cosmic isolation, hears never a voice but walks alone with his dreadful responsibility.

As for the knight of faith, he is assigned to himself alone, he has the pain of being unable to make himself intelligible to others but feels no vain desire to show others the way. The pain is the assurance, vain desires are unknown to him, his mind is too serious for that. The false knight readily betrays himself by this instantly acquired proficiency; he just doesn't grasp the point that if another individual is to walk the same path he has to be just as much the individual and is therefore in no need of guidance, least of all from one anxious to press his services on others. Here again, people unable to bear the martyrdom of unintelligibility jump off the path, and choose instead, conveniently enough, the world's admiration of their proficiency. The true knight of faith is a witness, never a teacher, and in this lies the deep humanity in him which is more worth than this foolish concern for others' weal and woe which is honoured under the name of sympathy, but which is really nothing but vanity. A person who wants only to be a witness confesses thereby that no one, not even the least, needs another person's sympathy, or is to be put down so another can raise himself up. But because what he himself won he did not win on the cheap, so neither does he sell it on the cheap; he is not so pitiable as to accept people's admiration and pay for it with silent contempt; he knows that whatever truly is great is available equally for all.

So either there is an absolute duty to God, and if so then it is the paradox described, that the single individual as the particular is higher than the universal and as the particular stands in an absolute relation to the absolute – or else faith has never existed because it has existed always; or else Abraham is done for; or else one must explain the passage in Luke 14 in the way that tasteful exegete did, and explain the corresponding passages likewise, and similar ones.

Problema III

Was it Ethically Defensible of Abraham to Conceal his Purpose from Sarah, from Eleazar, from Isaac?

The ethical is as such the universal; as the universal it is in turn the disclosed. Seen as an immediate, no more than sensate and psychic being, the individual is concealed. So his ethical task is to unwrap himself from this concealment and become disclosed in the universal. Thus whenever he wants to remain in concealment, he sins and is in a state of temptation, from which he can emerge only by disclosing himself.

We find ourselves again at the same point. Unless there is a concealment which has its basis in the single individual's being higher than the universal, then Abraham's conduct cannot be defended, since he disregarded the intermediate ethical considerations. If, however, there is such a concealment, then we face the paradox, which cannot be mediated, just because it is based on the single individual's being, in his particularity, higher than the universal, and it is precisely the universal that is the mediation. The Hegelian philosophy assumes there is no justified concealment, no justified incommensurability. It is therefore consistent in its requirement of disclosure, but it isn't quite fair and square in wanting to regard Abraham as the father of faith and to speak about faith. For faith is not the first immediacy but a later one. The first immediacy is the aesthetic, and here the Hegelian philosophy may well be right. But faith is not the aesthetic, or if it is, then faith has never existed just because it has existed always.

It will be best here to look at the whole matter in a purely aesthetic way and for that purpose embark on an aesthetic inquiry, which I would ask the reader for the time being to enter wholeheartedly into, while I for my part will adapt my presentation accordingly. The category I would like to examine a little more closely is that of the *interesting*, a category that especially today (just because we live *in discrimine rerum* [at a turning-point in human affairs]) has acquired great importance, for really it is the category of crisis. Therefore one should not, as sometimes happens, when one has been oneself enamoured of it *pro virili* [with all one's strength], disdain the category because it has passed one by; but neither should one be too greedy for it, for what is certain is that to become of interest, for one's life to be interesting, has nothing to do with what you can turn your hand to but is a fateful privilege which, like every privilege in the world of spirit, can only be purchased in deep pain. Thus Socrates was the most interesting person that has lived, his life the most interesting that has been led, but that existence was allotted to him by the deity, and since he had to work for it he was no stranger to trouble and pain. Taking such an existence in vain ill-becomes some-one who takes life seriously, and yet such attempts are nowadays not infrequently observed. The category of the interesting is, moreover, a borderline one, it marks the boundary between the aesthetic and the ethical. For that reason in our inquiry we must be constantly glancing over into the territory of ethics, while to give our inquiries weight the problem must be grasped with genuine aesthetic feeling. These days ethics rarely considers such things. The reason is supposed to be that there is no room for them in the System. But then doing so in monographs should be all right; and besides, if one doesn't want to be long-winded about it one can achieve the same results by being brief, so long as one has the predicate in one's power; for a predicate or two can reveal a whole world. Is there no room in the System for little words like these?

Aristotle says in his immortal *Poetics*: 'duo men oun tou muthou meri, peri taut' esti, peripeteia kai anagnorisis' (cf. Ch. 11) ['. . . indeed two parts in the myth, namely sudden change of fortune [the reverse (on which the plot of a tragedy turns)] and recognition, concern these things']. Naturally only the second feature, *anagnorisis*, recognition, concerns me here. Whenever there is recognition there is *eo ipso* a question of prior concealment. Just as the recognition is the resolving factor, or the element of relaxation in the life of drama, so is concealment the element of tension. What Aristotle says earlier in the same chapter in respect of the consequences for the worth of tragedy of the question whether *peripeteia* and *anagnorisis* clash, as well as of the 'single' and 'double' recognition, I cannot go into here, even though the sincerity and quiet absorption of Aristotle's discussion have an inevitable attraction for one long since tired of the superficial omniscience of the synopticists. A general observation must suffice. In Greek tragedy concealment (and therefore recognition) is an epic survival based on a fate in which the dramatic action disappears from view, and from which it acquires its obscure and enigmatic origin. This is why the effect produced by a Greek tragedy bears a resemblance to the impression given by a marble statue that lacks the power of the eye. Greek tragedy is blind. Hence it takes a certain abstraction to appreciate it. A son murders his father, but not until later learns it is his father. A sister is about to sacrifice her brother, but at the decisive moment discovers that is who it is. Tragedy of this nature is less apt to interest our *reflective* age. Modern drama has given up the idea of Fate, has in dramatic respects emancipated itself; it observes, it looks in upon itself, takes fate up into its dramatic consciousness. Concealment and disclosure then become the hero's free act, for which he is responsible.

Recognition and concealment are also an essential part of modern drama. It would take us too far to give examples. I am courteous enough to assume that everyone in this so aesthetically voluptuous age, so potent and aroused that conception occurs as easily as with the partridge which, Aristotle says, needs only to hear the voice of the cock or its flight overhead – to assume that at the mere sound of the word 'concealment' everyone can easily shake a dozen romances and comedies from his sleeve. I can therefore be brief and offer straightaway a fairly broad observation. If the person doing the hiding, i.e. the one who puts the dramatic yeast into the play, hides something nonsensical, we have comedy. But if the concealer is related to the idea, he may come close to being a tragic hero. To give just one example of the comic. A man puts on make-up and wears a wig. The same man wants to have success with the fair sex, and is sure enough of conquests with the help of the make-up and wig, which there is no doubt make him irresistible. He captures a girl and is on the pinnacle of joy. But now for the point. If he can admit his deception, will he not lose *all* of his powers of fascination once he is revealed as a quite ordinary, in fact even bald-headed male? Doesn't he have to lose the loved one again? Concealment is his free action, for which aesthetics holds him responsible. But that discipline is no friend of bald hypocrites, and will leave him to the mercy of our laughter. Let that suffice as a hint of what I mean, since we cannot include comedy in the terms of this investigation.

My procedure here must be to let concealment pass dialectically between aesthetics and ethics, for the point is to show how absolutely different the paradox and aesthetic concealment are from one another.

A few examples. A girl is secretly in love, though neither party has openly confessed its love to the other. Her parents force her to marry another (she may even be motivated out of considerations of duty). She obeys. She hides her love 'so as not to make the other unhappy, and no one will ever know what she suffers'. – Or a young lad is in a position, just by dropping one word, to possess the object of his craving and restless dreams. But that little word will compromise, yes, even, who knows, ruin an entire family. He nobly chooses to stay in conceal-ment, 'the girl must never know, so that she can perhaps find happiness with another'. What a pity that these two, both concealed from their respective loved ones, are also concealed from one another! For otherwise a remarkable higher unity might have been brought about. – Their concealment is a free act, for which even aesthetically they are responsible. However, aesthetics is a respectful and sentimental discipline which knows more ways of fixing things than any assistant house-manager. So what does it do? It does everything possible for the lovers. By means of a coincidence the respective partners in the projected marriages get wind of the other party's noble decision. Explanations follow. They get each other and as a bonus the rank of real heroes as well; for notwith-standing they have had no time even to sleep on their heroic resolutions, aesthetics sees it as if they had bravely fought for their goal over many years. For aesthetics doesn't bother much about time; it goes just as quickly whether in jest or earnest.

But ethics knows nothing either of this coincidence or this sentimentality. Nor does it have such a rapid concept of time. Thus the matter acquires a different complexion. You can't argue with ethics, because it uses pure cate-gories. It doesn't appeal to experience, which of all laughable things is perhaps the most laughable and, far from making a man wise, if he knows nothing higher it will sooner make him mad. Ethics has no coincidence, so no explanations follow; it doesn't flirt with thoughts of dignity, it puts an enormous burden of responsibility on the hero's frail shoulders; it condemns as presump-tuous his thought of wanting to play providence in his action, but also condemns him for wanting to do likewise with his suffering. It enjoins the belief in reality and the courage to contend with all its tribulations, rather than with those bloodless sufferings he has taken on himself by his own responsibility; it warns against putting faith in the calculating shrewdness of reason, more treacherous than the oracles of the ancients. It warns against all misplaced magnanimity. Let reality decide the occasion, that is the time to show courage. But then ethics, too, will offer every possible assistance. If something deeper had been stirring in those two, however, if there had been a seriousness to see the task, to set about it, then no doubt something would have come of them. But ethics cannot help them. Ethics is offended because they are keeping a secret from it, a secret they have incurred on their own responsibility.

Thus aesthetics called for concealment and rewarded it. Ethics called for disclosure and punished concealment.

Sometimes, however, even aesthetics calls for disclosure. When the hero held captive in the aesthetic illusion believes he can save another by his silence, aesthetics calls for silence and rewards it. But when the hero's action involves interfering in another person's life, it calls for disclosure. Now I am talking of the tragic hero. Consider for a moment Euripides's *Iphigenia in Aulis*. Agamemnon is about to sacrifice Iphigenia. Now aesthetics calls for Agamemnon's silence, in so far as it would be unworthy of the hero to seek another's consolation, just as he should keep it quiet as long as possible for the women's sake. On the other hand the hero, to be that, has also to be tested in the terrible temptation incurred by the tears of Clytemnestra and Iphigenia. What does aesthetics do? It has a way out; it has an old servant standing by who discloses everything to Clytemnestra. And now everything is as it should be.

Ethics, however, has no coincidence, and no old servant standing by. The aesthetic idea contradicts itself as soon as it is applied in reality. Ethics therefore demands disclosure. The tragic hero demonstrates exactly this ethical courage by, not himself being captive to the aesthetic illusion, taking it upon himself to tell Iphigenia her fate. In this the tragic hero is the beloved son of ethics, in whom she is well pleased. If he remains silent, it may be because by doing so he makes it easier for others, or it could also be because it makes it easier for himself. But the tragic hero knows he is free of the latter incentive. In keeping silent here he would be assuming responsibility as an individual, inasmuch as he is impervious to any argument from outside. But this, as tragic hero, he cannot do; for it is just in so far as he continues to express the universal that ethics loves him. His heroic action requires courage, but part of that courage is that he shirks no argument. Now tears, certainly, are a terrible *argumentum ad hominem*, and there are no doubt those whom nothing else touches but who can still be stirred by tears. The play lets Iphigenia weep, in fact like Jephthah's daughter she should have been allowed two months to weep, not in solitude but at her father's feet, to use all her art 'which is but tears', and twine herself instead of the olive branch about his knees (cf. v. 1224).

Aesthetics required disclosure but availed itself of a coincidence; ethics required disclosure and found satisfaction in the tragic hero.

For all the strictness of the ethical requirement of disclosure, it cannot be denied that secrecy and silence, as determinants of inner feeling, really make for greatness in a man. When Amor leaves Psyche he says to her, 'You will give birth to a child who will be divine if you say nothing, but human if you betray the secret.' The tragic hero, the darling of ethics, is a purely human being, and he is someone I can understand, someone all of whose undertakings are in the open. If I go further I always run up against the paradox, the divine and the demonic; for silence is both of these. It is the demon's lure, and the more silent one keeps the more terrible the demon becomes; but silence is also divinity's communion with the individual.

Before coming back to the story of Abraham, however, I would like to present some poetic personages. By exercising the power of dialectic over them I shall keep them at extremes, and by waving the scourge of despair over them I should prevent them from standing still, so that in their anguish they might perhaps bring something or other to light.*

---

* These movements and attitudes could also be handled aesthetically. But I leave it open how far faith and the life of belief in general can be handled in that way. I will only – since I always like to thank those to whom I owe something – express my gratitude to Lessing for the few hints of a Christian drama to be found in his *Hamburgische Dramaturgie*. But he has focused on the purely divine side of that life (the consummated victory), and has therefore despaired. Perhaps if he had paid more attention to the human side he would have come to a different conclusion. (*Theologia viatorum* [wayfarer's theology].) What he says is undeniably very brief, partly evasive, but as I am always very glad of the chance of Lessing's company I seize on it

Aristotle tells in his *Politics* of a political disturbance in Delphi, arising from a marriage. *The bridegroom, for whom the augurs had predicted a misfortune as a result of his forthcoming marriage, at the crucial moment, when he is to fetch the bride, suddenly changes his plans* – he won't go through with the wedding. That is all I need.* In Delphi this surely did not pass off without tears. If a poet took it up he could doubtless count on arousing sympathy. Is it not terrible that the love so often excluded in life should here also be deprived of the aid of heaven? Isn't the old proverb that marriages are made in heaven here put to shame? Usually it is the trials and tribulations of finitude which, like evil spirits, would separate the lovers,

---

immediately. Lessing was not just one of the most erudite minds Germany has produced; he was not just unusually exact in his learning, so that one can safely rely on him and his autopsy without fear of being tricked by inaccurate and concocted quotations, half-understood phrases taken from unreliable compendia, or of being put off-balance by a foolish advertising of novelties that the ancients have stated far better; he had in addition a most unusual gift for explaining what he himself had understood. There he stopped. Nowadays one goes further and explains more than one has understood.

* According to Aristotle the course of the catastrophe is as follows. In order to avenge itself, the [bride's] family plants a vase from the temple among the bridegroom's household belongings and he is condemned as a temple-robber. But this is immaterial, for the question is not whether the family is clever or stupid in the manner of its taking revenge; the family is of only theoretical interest in as much as it impinges on the dialectic of the hero. Besides, there is fatefulness enough in the fact that, though intending to avoid the danger by not marrying, he plunges right into it, together with the fact that his life comes into twofold contact with the divine, first in the utterance of the augur and second by his being condemned as a temple-robber.

while love itself has heaven on its side and this holy alliance overwhelms all foes. Here it is heaven itself that separates what heaven, after all, has joined together. Who would have guessed? The young bride least of all. A moment earlier she was sitting in her room in all her beauty, and the sweet young maids had adorned her with such care that they would be prepared to justify their handiwork before the whole world, that it gave them more than happiness, it even made them envious – yes, even happy that they couldn't be even more envious, since she could not have been more beautiful. Sitting there alone in her room she was then transfigured from one beauty to another; for all that a woman's art could accomplish had been turned virtuously to the embellishment of virtue. But there still lacked something the young girl had not dreamed of, a veil, finer, lighter, and yet more concealing than the one in which the young maids had enveloped her, a bridal gown no maid had knowledge of or could help her with, even the bride herself did not know how to put it on. It was an unseen, friendly influence which takes satisfaction in adorning a bride and wraps itself around her without her knowledge, for all she saw was the bridegroom walking by on his way to the temple. She saw the door close after him, and she became even more calm and blissful, for she knew that he now belonged to her more than ever. The temple door opened, he stepped out, but demurely she turned her gaze down and so did not see that his face was troubled. Yet he saw that heaven must be jealous of the bride's loveliness and of his good fortune. The temple door opened, the young maids saw the bridegroom step out, but they did not see that his face was troubled, for they were busy about bringing the bride. Then she came forward in all her maidenly modesty, and yet like a mistress surrounded by her *cortège* of young maids of honour, who curtsied before her as a young maid always curtsies before a bride. Thus at the head of her lovely troupe she stood and waited – it was but a moment, for the temple was close by – and the bridegroom came, but he passed by her door.

But here I break off. I am not a poet, I only practise dialectics. One should note first of all that it is at the crucial moment that the hero learns what is in store, so he is pure and blameless, hasn't bound himself irresponsibly to the loved one. Second, it is a divine utterance he has before him, or rather against him, so he is not ruled like those feeble lovers and sweethearts by conceit. Further, it goes without saying that this utterance makes him just as unhappy as the bride, indeed rather more so since after all he is the occasion. True, the augurs only predicted a misfortune for *him*, but the question is whether the misfortune is not of such a nature as to affect also their marital happiness. So what is he to do? (1) Is he to remain silent and get married and think 'Perhaps the misfortune won't come right away, and anyway I have been true to my love and not afraid to make myself unhappy; but I must remain silent, otherwise even the brief moment is lost.' This sounds plausible but is in fact by no means so, for in this he insults the girl. By keeping silent he has in a way made her guilty, for had she known the truth she would never have given her consent to such a union. So in the hour of need he will have to bear not only the misfortune but also the responsibility for not having said anything, as well as her righteous anger at his not having said anything. (2) Is he to remain silent and not get married? In that case he must enter into a deception in which he annihilates himself in his relation to her. Aesthetics might approve of this. The catastrophe could then be fashioned as in the real story except that at the last moment there would be explanations, though too late since aesthetically it will be necessary to let him die, unless that discipline can see its way to revoking the fateful prophecy. Yet, noble as this conduct may be, it involves an insult to the girl and the reality of her love. (3) Is he to speak? Naturally one mustn't forget that our hero is a little too poetic for the giving up of his love to have no importance except as an unsuccessful business venture. If he speaks, then the whole thing becomes an unfortunate love-story in the vein of Axel and Valborg. They will be a couple whom heaven itself puts asunder. Nevertheless in the present case this separation is to be conceived somewhat differently, since it, too, is also the result of the free acts of the individuals. For what is so very difficult with the dialectic in this case is that the misfortune is to affect only him. These two, then, do not find a common expression of their suffering, as do Axel and Valborg, whom heaven separates equally from each other because they are equally close to each other.* If that were the

---

* Here one might trace the dialectic movements in a different direction. Heaven predicts a personal misfortune due to the marriage, so he could just as well give up the marriage yet needn't give up the girl on that account, but live in a romantic relationship with her

case here, a way out could be found. For since heaven uses no visible power to separate them, but leaves it to them, one could well imagine that they ended united in defiance of heaven together with its misfortune.

Ethics, however, will require him to speak. The essence of his valour in that case is to be found in his giving up his aesthetic high-mindedness, which here could hardly be thought to contain any admixture of the vanity connected with concealment, since it must be clear to him that he still makes the girl unhappy. The

---

which was more than satisfactory for the lovers. This, however, amounts to insulting the girl, for in his love for her he doesn't express the universal, and it was the task both of the poet and of the ethicist to defend marriage. On the whole, were poetry to attend to the religious aspect and to the inner feeling of its characters, it would command themes of much greater importance than those it now occupies itself with. Here is the story poetry is repeatedly giving us: a man is stuck with a girl he once loved, or maybe never really loved because he has now seen another who is the ideal. A man makes mistakes in life, it was the right street but the wrong house, for on the second floor just over the way lives the ideal – that's what people consider the proper subject of poetry. A lover makes a mistake, he saw his loved one by candlelight and thought she had dark hair, but look!, on closer inspection she was blonde – however, the sister, there's the ideal. That's what people think poetry is about. In my view any such man is an impudent fool who can be unbearable enough in life but should be instantly booed off the stage when he tries to put on airs in poetry. Only the clash of passion against passion provides a poetic collision, not this rummaging about in the particulars of the same passion. In the Middle Ages, for example, when a girl has fallen in love and then been convinced that earthly love is a sin and prefers a heavenly love, here we have a poetic collision; and the girl too is poetic, for her life is in the idea.

reality of this heroism is based, however, on its having had and cancelled its presupposition [that he genuinely loved her and kept quiet for her sake and not his – translator's addition]; for otherwise we would get heroes enough, particularly in our own time which has acquired a matchless proficiency in the forgery that does the highest by skipping over what lies in between.

But why this sketch if I nevertheless come no further than the tragic hero? Because it might still throw light on the paradox. That all depends on our hero's relationship to that utterance of the augur's, which in one way or another is going to decide the course of his life. Is this utterance *publici juris* [public property] or is it a *privatissimum* [private matter]? The scene is laid in Greece; an augur's utterance is intelligible to all – I don't mean just in the sense that the individual can grasp the content lexically, but that the individual can understand that what an augur is conveying to him is a decision of heaven's. So the augur's utterance is intelligible not just to the hero but to everyone and results in no private relation to the divine. Turn where he will, what was prophesied will happen, and neither by doing anything nor by refraining from doing anything will he come into a closer relationship with the divine, become an object either of divine mercy or of divine wrath. The outcome will be as understandable to anyone as to the hero, and there is no secret writing that only the hero can read. So should he want to speak he can perfectly well do so, for he can make himself understood; and if he wants to remain silent it is because he wants, by virtue of being the single individual, to be higher than the universal, wants to delude himself with all manner of phantasies about how she will soon forget this sorrow, etc. On the other hand, if the will of heaven had not been announced to him by an augur, if it had been made known to him in some quite private way, if it had placed itself in a quite private relationship to him, then we are with the paradox – supposing there is such a thing (since my reflections here have the form of a dilemma) – then he could not speak however much he might wish to. He would not enjoy his own silence but suffer the pain, yet for him just this would be the assurance he needed that he did right. So the reason for his silence would not be a wish to place himself as the single individual in an absolute relation to the *universal*, but to be placed as the single individual in an absolute relationship to the *absolute*. In this, so far as I can tell, he would also be able to find repose, whereas the requirements of the ethical would be constantly disturbing his high-minded silence. One only wishes that aesthetics might try to start where for so many years it has ended, with the illusion of high-mindedness. As soon as it did so it would work hand in hand with religion, for that is the only power capable of rescuing the aesthetic from its conflict with the ethical. Queen Elizabeth sacrifices to the State her love for Essex by signing his death-warrant. That was a deed of heroism, even if some private resentment had a hand in it because he hadn't sent her the ring. We know that he did send it, but it was held back through the malice of some lady-in-waiting. Elizabeth is said, *ni fallor* [if I am not mistaken], to have been informed of this, and sat for ten days with one finger in her mouth, biting it without saying a word, and then she died. That would be something for a poet who knew how to wrench open the mouth; otherwise it would be of use at best to a ballet master, with whom nowadays the poet no doubt too often confuses himself.

I now want to follow this by a sketch along the lines of the demonic. For this I shall use the legend of *Agnete and the Merman*. The merman is a seducer who rises up from concealment in the depths, and in wild desire grasps and breaks the innocent flower standing in all its charm by the shore, pensively bending its head to the ocean's roar. That is what the poets have so far made of it. Let us make a change. The merman was a seducer. He has called out to Agnete, with his smooth talk has coaxed from her her secret thoughts. She has found in the merman what she was seeking, what she gazed down to find in the depths of the sea. Agnete is willing to follow him down. The merman has taken her into his arms, Agnete twines hers about his neck trustingly and with all her soul she abandons herself to the stronger one. He is already at the sea-edge, bending over the water to dive down with his prey. Then Agnete looks at him again, not fearfully, not questioningly, not proud of her good luck, not intoxicated with desire, but in absolute faith, with absolute humility, like the humble flower she deemed herself to be; with absolute confidence she entrusts to him her entire fate. – And look! The ocean roars no more, its wild voice is stilled, nature's passion – which is the merman's strength – deserts him, the sea becomes dead calm. And still Agnete is looking at him in this way. Then the merman collapses, he is unable to resist the power of innocence, his element becomes unfaithful to him, he cannot seduce Agnete. He leads her home again, he explains to her that he only wanted to show her how beautiful the sea is when it is calm, and Agnete believes him. Then he turns back alone, and the ocean rages, but more wildly still rages the merman's despair. He can seduce Agnete, he can seduce hundreds of Agnetes, he can charm any girl – but Agnete has triumphed and the merman has lost her. Only as his prize can she become his; he cannot belong faithfully to any girl, for he is only a merman. I have allowed myself a slight modification* in the merman. In fact I have

---

* There is still another way of treating this legend. The merman does not want to seduce Agnete, even though he has seduced many previously. He is no longer a merman, or is if you will a pitiable merman who has now already for some time been sitting sorrowfully on the sea-bed. However, he knows (as indeed the legend has it) that he can be saved by an innocent girl's love. But he has a bad conscience about girls and dare not approach them. Then he sees Agnete. Already, many times, as he lay hidden in the reeds, he has seen her walking along the shore. Her beauty, her quiet self-possession captivate him; but his soul is filled with sadness, no wild desire rages there. And when the merman blends his sigh with the whispering of the reeds she turns her ear towards it. Then she stands still and falls into reverie, more delectable than any woman and yet beautiful as an angel of deliverance, who inspired the merman with confidence. The merman plucks up courage, he approaches Agnete, he wins her love, he hopes for his deliverance. But Agnete was no quiet girl, she was in fact very taken with the roaring of the ocean and what pleased her about the sad sighing by the sea was that it made the roar in her breast grow stronger. She would be off and away, rush wildly out into the infinite with the merman, whom she loves – so she eggs the merman on. She scorned his humility and now the pride reawakens.

slightly altered Agnete too. In the legend Agnete is by no means guiltless – and in general it is nonsense and sheer coquetry as well as an insult to the female sex to imagine a seduction where the girl is in no way, in no way at all, to blame. In the legend Agnete is, to modernize my expression somewhat, a woman who hankers for 'the interesting', and one such can always be certain there is a merman in the offing; for mermen keep a weather-eye open for the likes of these and they make for them like a shark for its prey. It is therefore very foolish to suppose (or is it a rumour spread abroad by the merman?) that so-called refinement protects a girl from seduction. No, life is more just and fair, there is only one means of protection, it is innocence.

We will now give the merman a human consciousness, and let his being a merman indicate a human pre-existence in the consequences of which his life has become entangled. There is nothing to prevent his being a hero; for the step he now takes is reconciliatory. He is saved by Agnete, the seducer is crushed, he has bowed to the power of innocence, he can never seduce again. But immediately two powers claim control of him: repentance [alone] and repentance with Agnete. If repentance alone takes possession of him he remains

---

And the sea roars and the waves foam, and the merman embraces Agnete, and dives with her into the depths. Never had he been so wild, never so full of desire; for with this girl he had hoped for his deliverance. Before long he became tired of Agnete, but her body was never found; for she became a mermaid, who tempted men with her songs.

concealed, if repentance and Agnete take possession of him he is disclosed.

Now in so far as repentance alone grips the merman and he remains concealed, then he must certainly make Agnete unhappy; for Agnete loved him in all her innocence, she believed him that moment when even to her he seemed changed, however well he concealed it, and said he only wanted to show her the beautiful calm of the sea. However, as far as passion is concerned, the merman himself becomes even more unhappy; for he loved Agnete with a multiplicity of passions and has a new guilt to bear besides. The demonic side of repentance will now no doubt explain to him that this is precisely his punishment, and the more it torments him the better.

If he gives in to this demonic possibility, he may make one more attempt to save Agnete, in the way one can in a sense save someone by resort to evil. He knows Agnete loves him. If he can only tear this love away from her she will in a way be saved. But how to do that? The merman has too much sense to reckon that a candid confession will arouse her disgust. Then perhaps he will try to arouse all dark passions in her, scorn her, mock her, hold her love up to ridicule, if possible stir up her pride. He will spare himself no torment, for this is the deep contradiction in the demonic and in a sense there dwells infinitely more good in a demonic than in a superficial person. The more selfish Agnete is, the more easily she will be deceived (only those with very little experience think it easy to deceive innocence, life is very profound and it is the astute who find it easiest to trick one another), but all the more terribly the merman will suffer. The more ingeniously contrived his deception the less will Agnete bashfully hide her own pain from him; she will use every means, not without effect, not, that is, to shake him loose but to torment him.

By means of the demonic the merman would thus aspire to be the single individual who as the particular is higher than the universal. The demonic has that same property as the divine, that the individual can enter into an absolute relationship to it. This is the analogue, the counterpart to the paradox we are discussing. It therefore bears a certain resemblance to it that can prove misleading. Thus the merman apparently has the proof of the justification of his silence that it is because of it that he suffers all his pain. However, there is no doubt that he can speak. So he can be a tragic hero, to my mind a tragic hero on the grand scale, if he does speak. Perhaps only few will understand what the grandeur consists in.*

---

* Aesthetics sometimes treats a similar theme with its usual captiousness. The merman is saved through Agnete and all ends in a happy marriage. A happy marriage! Very handy, to be sure. On the other hand if ethics is to give the wedding speech I imagine things would go differently. Aesthetics throws the cloak of love over the merman and so everything is forgotten. It is also rash enough to suppose that things happen at a wedding as they do at an auction, where everything is sold in the condition it is in when it comes under the hammer. All it cares for is that the lovers get one another, the rest is of no concern. If only it could see what happens afterwards! But it hasn't time for that, straightaway it is in full swing again snapping together another couple. Aesthetics is the most faithless of all sciences. Anyone who has truly loved it will in a way become unhappy; while anyone who has never done so is and will remain a *pecus* [ox, or blockhead].

He will then have the courage to free himself of all self-deception about being able to make Agnete happy by his art; he will have the courage to crush Agnete, humanly speaking. Here I will just add a psychological observation. The more selfish we make Agnete, the more effective the self-deception will be, indeed it is not inconceivable that with his demonic astuteness a merman might in reality not only have, humanly speaking, saved Agnete but brought something exceptional out of her. A demon knows how to torture powers out of even the weakest person, and in his way he can have the best intentions towards a human being.

The merman stands at a dialectical extremity. If he is saved from the demonic side of repentance two paths are possible. He can hold himself back, remain in hiding, but not depend on his astuteness. In that case he does not come as the single individual into an absolute relation to the demonic, but finds repose in the counter-paradox that the divine will save Agnete. (This is how the movement would have been made in the Middle Ages, for on its conception the merman has obviously dedicated himself to the monastery.) Or else he can be saved through Agnete. Now this must not be understood as meaning that Agnete's love might save him from being a seducer in the future (that is an aesthetic rescue attempt, which always avoids the main issue, namely the continuity in the merman's life); in that respect he is already saved. He will be saved in so far as he is disclosed. So he marries Agnete. But he must still resort to the paradox. For when through his own guilt the individual has come out of the universal, he can only return to it on the strength of having come, as the particular, into an absolute relation to the absolute. Here I will insert a comment which takes us further than anything that has been said anywhere in the foregoing.* Sin is not the first immediacy, sin is a later immediacy. In sin the individual is already in terms of the demonic paradox higher than the universal, because it is a contradiction on the part of the universal to want to impose itself on someone who lacks the *conditio sine qua non* [the necessary condition]. Should philosophy, amongst its other conceits, imagine that someone might actually want to follow its precepts in practice, a curious comedy would emerge. An ethics that ignores sin is an altogether futile discipline, but once it postulates sin it has *eo ipso* [thereby] gone beyond itself. Philosophy tells us that the immediate is to be superseded [*ophœvet*, German *aufgehoben*]. True enough, but what is not true is that sin, any more than faith, is without further ado the immediate.

Everything goes smoothly so long as I move in these spheres, but in fact not even what is said here helps to explain Abraham. He did not become the single individual through sin; on the contrary he was that righteous man who is God's chosen. So any analogy with Abraham will only surface after the individual has become capable of

---

* Up to this point I have carefully avoided all consideration of the question of sin and its reality. Everything has been centred on Abraham, and he can still be reached with the categories of immediacy, at least so far as I can understand him. But once sin makes its appearance ethics comes to grief precisely on the question of repentance. Repentance is the highest ethical expression but for that very reason the most profound ethical self-contradiction.

accomplishing the universal, and now the paradox is repeated.

I can therefore understand the movements of the merman, but I cannot understand Abraham. It is to realize the universal that the merman has recourse to the paradox. If he stays hidden and dedicates himself to all the torments of repentance, he becomes a demon, and as such is brought to nothing. If he stays hidden but entertains no clever thoughts about being able to extricate Agnete at the cost of his own torment in the bondage of repentance, he will no doubt find peace but is lost to the world. If he discloses himself, lets himself be saved through Agnete, then he is the greatest human being I can imagine. It is only aesthetics which irresponsibly thinks it can praise the power of love by letting the lost man be loved by an innocent girl and saved thereby. Only aesthetics mistakes what it sees and thinks the girl rather than the merman is the hero. So the merman cannot belong to Agnete before, after making the infinite movement of repentance, he has made one more movement, that on the strength of the absurd. His own strength suffices for the movement of repentance, but it calls for absolutely all his energies, and it is therefore impossible for him by his own strength to return and grasp reality. If one lacks sufficient passion to make either movement, when one scrimps through life, repenting a little and thinking the rest will take care of itself, one has given up living in the idea once and for all, and then it is very easy to reach, and help others reach, the highest; i.e. delude oneself and others with the notion that the world of spirit is like *Gnavspil* [a card game], where everyone cheats. So one can amuse oneself by reflecting how strange it is that just in an age when everyone can reach the highest there should be such widespread doubt about the immortality of the soul; since even someone who has only, but genuinely, made the movement of infinity can scarcely be called a doubter. The conclusions of passion are the only reliable, i.e. the only convincing, ones. Fortunately life is in this case more kindly, more faithful, than the wise would have it. It excludes no one, not even the humblest; it tricks nobody, for in the world of spirit the only people who are tricked are those who trick themselves. It is the general opinion, and as far as I dare be my own judge, also my own, that entering the monastery is not the highest. But I by no means believe on that account that the fact that nobody goes into monasteries today means that we are all greater than those profound and earnest souls who found repose there. How many people are there now with the passion to think this thought and then judge themselves honestly? The very idea of thus taking time on one's conscience, of giving conscience time to search out with its sleepless perseverance every secret thought, so that unless one is making the movement every instant on the strength of what is noblest and most holy in a human being one can discover with anguish and horror,* and call forth by anguish itself

---

* This is not credited in our serious age, and yet remarkably enough even in the typically flightier and less consistently reflective age of paganism the two representatives of the Greek *gnothi sauton* [know thyself] way of thought have, each in his own manner, intimated that if one probes one's own depths what one uncovers is first and foremost the disposition to evil. I need hardly remark that I am thinking of Pythagoras and Socrates.

if by nothing else, the dark passions which after all lie concealed in every human life, whereas living in society with others one so easily forgets, so easily avoids, is in so many ways held above all this, gets the chance to start again – this very idea, grasped with decent respect, I would have thought could in itself chasten many an individual in this age of ours which thinks it has already reached the highest. Yet such things worry people little in this age that thinks it has reached the heights, though no age has fallen so much victim to the comic than ours. Indeed it is hard to grasp why it hasn't already given birth, by a *generatio æquivoca* [spontaneous generation], to its hero, that demon who will stage without scruple that horrifying play that reduces the whole age to laughter and to unconsciousness of the fact that it is laughing at itself. Indeed what more is life worth than to be laughed at when people have already reached the highest by the time they are twenty? And yet what higher movement has the age come up with since people gave up entering monasteries? Is it not a contemptible worldliness, a circumspection and pusillanimity that sits at the head of the table, cravenly making people think they have reached the highest, and even slyly dissuading them from trying anything less? A person who has made the monastery movement has only one movement to go, that of the absurd. How many nowadays understand what the absurd is, how many live in such a way as to have renounced or gained everything, how many are even simply honest enough to know what they are and what they can and cannot do? And is it not true that if there are such, they are mostly to be found among the less educated and in part among women? Just as a demonic person always reveals himself without understanding himself, our age betrays its own defects in a kind of clairvoyance, for it is always calling for the comical. If that was really what it needed then perhaps the theatre would need a new play in which someone's dying for love was treated as comedy. Or would it not be better for our age if that were really to happen, if it were actually to witness such an occurrence, so that it might acquire the courage to believe in the power of spirit, the courage to stop abjectly stifling its better impulses, stop jealously stifling them in others – with laughter? Does the age really need a ridiculous *Erscheinung* [appearance, show] of an enthusiast in order to have something to laugh at? Or does it not rather need such an enthusiastic figure in reality to remind it of what it has forgotten?

If one wants a scenario along similar lines but more moving because the passion of repentance is not awakened, one can use a story from the Book of Tobit. The young Tobias wishes to marry Sarah, the daughter of Raguel and Edna. But the girl is surrounded in tragedy. She has been betrothed to seven men all of whom have died in the bride's house. For my scenario this is a flaw in the story, since there is something almost irresistibly comical in the thought of a girl's seven vain attempts to get married, although so near success, as near as a student who fails his finals seven times. The Book of Tobit places the accent elsewhere and that makes the high number important and in a certain sense even contributes to the tragic effect. It enhances the young Tobias's high-mindedness, partly because he is his parents' only son (6.14), partly because the deterrent obtrudes the more strongly. So this feature must be omitted. Sarah, then, is a girl who has never been in love, who still nurtures a young girl's notion of bliss, her immense mortgage in life, her *Vollmachtbrief zum Glücke* [authorization for happiness] – to love a man with all her heart. And yet she is the most unhappy of all, for she knows that the evil demon that loves her will kill the bridegroom on the wedding night. I have read of much sorrow, but I doubt if anywhere there is a sorrow as deep as that residing in the life of that girl. Nevertheless when the misfortune comes from outside there is a certain consolation. If life fails to bring a person what would make him happy, it is still a comfort that he could have received it. But the unfathomable sorrow which no time can disperse, no time heal, is to know that it would be no use even if life were to do everything! A Greek author conceals so infinitely much in his crude *naïveté* when he says: '*pantos gar oudeis Erota epfugen i feuksetai mechri an kallos i kai ofthalmoi Bleposin*' ['. . . for certainly no one has yet altogether escaped love, and none shall so long as there is beauty and eyes to see'] (cf. *Longi Pastoralia*). Many a girl has been made unhappy in love, but she *became* unhappy; Sarah *was* so before she became it. It is hard enough that one should not find the one to whom one can devote oneself, but *unspeakably* hard to be unable to devote oneself. A young girl surrenders herself to someone and then she is said no longer to be free, but Sarah was never free and yet never surrendered herself to anyone. It is hard enough that a girl should surrender herself to someone and be deceived by her love, but Sarah was deceived before she surrendered herself. What world of sorrow is not contained in what follows, when at length Tobias wishes to marry Sarah! What wedding-rites, what preparations! No girl was ever cheated as Sarah. She was cheated of the most blessed of all things, the absolute wealth which even the poorest girl possesses, cheated of the secure, unbounded, unfettered, unbridled self-surrender of devotion. For first there had to be the ritual of purification by placing the heart of a fish and its liver on glowing embers. And what a mother's leave-taking of the daughter who, just as she herself has been cheated of everything, must also cheat her own mother of *her* most beautiful possession. One just reads the narrative. Edna prepared the chamber and brought Sarah into it and wept, and she received the tears of her daughter – and said to her, 'My child, take heart. The Lord of heaven and earth may exchange your sorrow for joy. Daughter, take heart.' And now the moment for the wedding. We read on, if we can for tears: 'But when the door was shut and they were together, Tobias rose from the bed and said, "Rise up, sister, and we will pray that the Lord may have mercy on us"' (8.4).

Were a poet to read this story and use it, I wager a hundred to one he would place all the emphasis on the young Tobias. The heroism of being willing to risk his life in such obvious danger, of which the narrative reminds us once again, for the morning after the wedding Raguel says to Edna: 'Send one of the maids to see if he is still alive, so that, if not, we can bury him and no one will know it' (cf. 8.13) – this heroism would have been the theme for the poet. I venture to propose another. Certainly Tobias acted gallantly, resolutely, and chivalrously, but any man who lacks courage to do that is a milksop who knows neither what love is nor what it is to be a man, nor what is worth living for. He has not even grasped the little mystery that it is better to give than to receive, and has no inkling of what the great mystery is, namely that it is much harder to receive than to give, that is if one has had the courage to go without and did not prove a coward in the hour of need. No, Sarah is the heroine. Her I would like to draw close to as I have drawn close to no other girl, or been tempted to draw close in thought to anyone of whom I have read. For what love for God it takes to want to be healed when one has been crippled from the start for no fault of one's own, an unsuccessful specimen of humanity from the very beginning! What ethical maturity to take on the responsibility of allowing the loved one such an act of daring! What humility before another person! What faith in God that in the next instant she should not hate the man to whom she owed everything!

Let Sarah be a man and the demonic will not be far away. A proud and noble nature can endure everything, but one thing it cannot endure, it cannot endure pity. Pity implies an indignity that for such a person can only be inflicted from above, for in himself he can never become an object of pity. If he has sinned he can endure the punishment without despairing, but to be singled out from his mother's womb as an object of pity, a sweet fragrance in pity's nostrils, that he cannot bear. Pity has a curious dialectic; one moment it calls for guilt, the next it wants to do away with it, and so to be predestined to pity is the more dreadful the greater the individual's misfortune lies in the direction of the spiritual. But no guilt attaches to Sarah, she is thrown as a prey to every suffering and on top of that has to be tortured by human sympathy, for even I who admire her more than Tobias loves her, even I cannot mention her name without exclaiming 'The poor girl!' Let a man take Sarah's place, let him know that if he is to love a girl an infernal spirit will come and murder her on the wedding night, then he would certainly be likely to choose the demonic, shut himself up in himself and say in his heart, as does the demonic nature, 'Thanks, I am no friend of ceremony and fuss, I don't at all insist on the pleasures of love, I can just as well be a Bluebeard who gets his pleasure seeing girls die on their wedding night.' One generally hears very little about the demonic, in spite of this territory's having a peculiarly valid claim to discovery in our time, and notwithstanding that once he knows how to establish a certain rapport with the demon an observer can, at least in some respect or other, use almost anyone as an example. In this respect Shakespeare is and will always remain a hero. That horrid demon, the most demonic figure Shakespeare ever portrayed, and did so incomparably, Gloucester (later Richard III), what made him a demon? Obviously that he could not endure the pity that had been piled on him from childhood. His monologue in the first act of *King Richard III* is worth more than all moral systems, none of which bears a hint of the terrors of existence and of their nature.

I, that am rudely stamped, and want love's majesty
To strut before a wanton ambling nymph;
I, that am curtailed of this fair proportion,
Cheated of feature by dissembling nature,
Deformed, unfinished, sent before my time
Into this breathing world scarce half made up,
And that so lamely and unfashionable
That dogs bark at me as I halt by them . . .

Natures like Gloucester's cannot be saved by mediating them into an idea of society. Ethics really only makes fun of them, just as it would make a mockery of Sarah if it were to say to her, 'Why don't you express the universal and get married?' Such natures are aboriginally in the paradox, and they are by no means less perfect than others; it is only that they are either damned in the demonic paradox or delivered in the divine. Now people have been pleased to think from time immemorial that witches, gnomes, trolls, etc. are misshapen creatures, and it is undeniable that we all have a tendency when we see a misshapen person directly to link this idea with that of moral perversion. But what colossal injustice! It should really be the other way around. It is life itself that has corrupted them, as a stepmother makes degenerates of her stepchildren. To be put outside the universal from the start, by nature or by historical circumstance, that is the beginning of the demonic, and the individual can hardly be blamed for that. So Cumberland's Jew is also a demon notwithstanding his beneficence. Thus the demonic can also express itself in contempt for men, a contempt which it should nevertheless be noted does not make the demonic person himself act contemptuously; on the contrary his strength is his knowledge that he is better than all who pass judgement on him. – On all such matters the poets should be the first to make a stir. God knows what books our young versifiers are reading these days! Their studies are no doubt confined to learning rhymes by rote. Heaven knows what importance they have in life! Just now I couldn't honestly tell you whether they are good for anything but to give us edifying proof of the immortality of the soul, to the extent at least that one can safely say of them what Baggesen says of the city's poet, Kildevalle: 'if he is immortal then we all are'. – What has been said here about Sarah, almost in the style of a poetic production, appealing therefore in effect only to the imagination, finds its full significance if out of psychological interest one probes the meaning of the old saying: *'nullum unquam exstitit magnum ingenium sine aliqua dementia'* ['there was never great genius without some madness']. For the *dementia* here is the genius's suffering in life, is the expression, if I may say so, of divine jealousy, while genius itself is the mark of divine favour. Thus the genius is disorientated from the start in relation to the universal and put into relation to the paradox, whether, in despair over his own limitation, which in his own eyes turns his omnipotence into impotence, he seeks a demonic reassurance and therefore will not admit the limitation to either God or man, or he reassures himself religiously in love for the divine. There are psychological topics here to which it seems to me one could happily devote a lifetime, and yet we so rarely hear a word about them. How is madness related to genius? Can the one be constructed out of the other? In what sense and to what extent is the genius master of his own madness? For it goes without saying that to some degree he is indeed its master, otherwise he would really be mad. Performing such observations requires, however, a high order of ingenuity as well as love, since performing observations on people of superior talent is extremely difficult. If one bears this in mind in reading some of those authors most celebrated for their genius, it is conceivable that one might just, once in a while, though only with great effort, find out something.

I would like to consider one more case of an individual wanting to save the universal by his concealment and silence. I shall take the legend of *Faust*. Faust is a doubter,* an apostate of the spirit who goes the way of

---

* If one would rather not use a doubter, a similar figure would do. An ironist, for example, whose sharp eye has taken radical measure of the ludicrousness of life, who through a secret understanding with the forces of life ascertains what the patient needs. He knows he commands the power of laughter; should he wish to wield it he would be sure of victory and, what is even better, of his happiness. He knows some voice is going to raise itself against him, but also that he himself is the stronger; he knows people can still be brought for a moment to appear serious – but also that, privately, they long to laugh with him; he knows that it is still possible to bring a woman for a moment to hold up her fan before her eyes when she speaks, but he also knows that behind the fan she is laughing, he knows the fan is not completely opaque, he knows one can make invisible inscriptions on it, he knows that when a woman strikes at him with the fan it is because she has understood him, he knows infallibly how laughter creeps into a person and dwells there secretly, and how once lodged there it lies in ambush and waits. Let us suppose such an

the flesh. This is how the poets see it, and although it is repeated over and over again that every age has its Faust, poets still doggedly follow one another down this same beaten path. Let us make a slight change. Faust is a doubter *kat'eksochen* [in an eminent sense]; but he has a sympathetic nature. Even in Goethe's understanding of Faust I miss a deeper psychological insight into the secret conversations which doubt has with itself. Nowadays, when indeed all have experienced doubt, no poet has as yet made a move in this direction. I could think of offering them Royal Securities to write on, to put down 'all' they have experienced in this regard – for it is unlikely that what they have to say will take more than the left-hand margin.

Aristophanes, such a Voltaire, slightly altered, for he is also of a sympathetic nature, he loves life, loves people, and knows that even if a young, saved generation might benefit from the rebuke of laughter, in his own age for many it would mean rack and ruin. So he keeps silent and as far as possible forgets to laugh himself. But does he dare keep silent? Perhaps many will fail to see the difficulty I am referring to. They will probably consider it admirably high-minded of him to keep silent. That is not at all what I think. I believe that if any such person has not the magnanimity to keep silent he is a traitor to life. So I require this magnanimity of him. But if he has it he dares to keep silent. Ethics is a dangerous science and it may well have been out of purely ethical considerations that Aristophanes decided to let laughter pass judgement on his misguided age. Aesthetic magnanimity cannot help. Its account has no credit column for the taking of such risks. If he is silent he must enter the paradox. – Still another scenario: suppose, for example, someone is in possession of an explanation of a public hero's life, but one that explains it in a deplorable light, and yet a whole generation rests secure in this hero and has no suspicion of anything of the sort.

Only when one turns Faust back in on himself in this way – only then can the doubt appear poetically, only then does he himself genuinely discover in reality all its sufferings. Then he knows it is spirit that sustains life, but he also knows that the security and happiness people live in are not supported by the power of spirit but can be readily explained as unreflective bliss. As a doubter, as *the* doubter, he is above all that, and if someone wants to deceive him into supposing that he had put doubt behind him, he easily sees through that. One who has made a movement in the world of spirit, hence an infinite movement, can tell at once from the spoken line whether the speaker is a man of experience or a Münchhausen. What a Tamerlane could do with his Huns, Faust knows he can do with his doubt – frighten people out of their wits, make the very world shake under their feet, send people scattering in every direction, and cause the cry of alarm to sound from every quarter. And if he does that he is still not a Tamerlane, for having the warrant of thought he is in a sense authorized to act in this way. But Faust has a sympathetic nature, he loves life, his soul knows no envy, he sees he would be unable to prevent the landslide that would no doubt be set in motion, he has no wish for Herostratic honour – he remains silent, he hides his doubt in his soul more assiduously than the girl the fruit of her sinful love beneath her heart, he tries as well as he can to walk in step with others, but as far as what goes on inside him, that he consumes internally and in this way he makes himself a sacrifice to the universal.

Sometimes, when some eccentric raises the whirlwind

of doubt, one hears the complaint: 'If only he had kept quiet.' Faust too represents this notion. Anyone with any idea of what it means to live on spirit knows also what the hunger of doubt means, and that the doubter hungers just as much for the daily bread of life as for the sustenance of spirit. Even though all the pain Faust suffers can be a fairly good argument for its not being pride that possesses him, I shall nevertheless avail myself of a small precautionary device which is easy enough for me to come by, who, just as Gregory of Rimini was called *tortor infantium* because he subscribed to the damnation of infants, might be tempted to call myself *tortor heroum* – I am very inventive when it comes to torturing heroes. Faust sees Marguerite – not after he has chosen the life of pleasure, since my Faust doesn't choose pleasure at all – he sees Marguerite not in Mephistopheles's concave mirror but in all her lovable innocence, and because his soul has preserved its love for humankind he can also very well fall in love with her. But he is a doubter, his doubt has destroyed reality for him. So ideal is my Faust that he is not one of those scientific doubters who doubt for an hour every term at the lectern but can otherwise do anything, as indeed they do without the help of spirit or on its strength. He is a doubter, and the doubter hungers as much for his daily slice of joy as for the nourishment of spirit. But still he stays true to his decision, is silent, and talks to no one of his doubt, nor to Marguerite of his love.

It goes without saying that Faust is too ideal a figure to be satisfied with the tattle that if he spoke he would only set a more general discussion in motion, or that the whole affair would blow over without consequences, or perhaps this or perhaps that. (Here, as will be obvious to any poet, lies the dormant comedy in our scenario, bringing Faust into ironical relation to those slapstick fools who nowadays chase after doubt, produce an external argument, e.g. a doctor's certificate, to show that they have really doubted, or take an oath that they have doubted everything, or else prove it by the fact that on their journey they met up with a doubter – those express couriers and sprint-experts in the world of spirit who in all haste gather a little hint of doubt from this person and a little hint of faith from that, and then *wirtschafte* [do business] as best they may depending on whether the congregation wants fine sand or coarse sand.) Faust is too ideal a figure to walk about in slippers. No one who lacks an infinite passion is ideal and anyone who does have an infinite passion has long since saved his soul from such rubbish. He is silent so as to offer himself – or else he talks, well knowing that he will put everything into confusion.

He is silent, so ethics condemns him. It says: 'You must acknowledge the universal, and you do that by speaking, and you dare not take pity on the universal.' This is something one should not forget when one sometimes judges a doubter severely for speaking. I myself am not inclined to judge such conduct leniently, but here as everywhere it is a question of the movements occurring properly. If things go wrong, then a doubter, even if by speaking he should bring all manner of misfortune upon the world, would still be far preferable to these miserable sweet-tooths who try a taste of everything and would cure doubt without being acquainted with it, and are therefore as a rule the immediate cause of outbreaks of ungoverned and unmanageable doubt. – If he speaks he confuses everything, for if nothing happens he only finds that out afterwards, and the consequence can be of no help either in the moment of acting or in questions of responsibility.

If he is silent on his own responsibility, he may indeed be acting magnanimously, but to his other pains there is added a little temptation. The universal will be forever plaguing him and saying, 'You should have spoken, how can you be certain that it wasn't after all some hidden pride that prompted your decision?'

If on the other hand the doubter can be the single individual who as the particular stands in an absolute relation to the absolute, then he receives authorization for his silence. But then he must make guilt of his doubt. But then he is in the paradox. But then his doubt is cured, even though he can acquire another.

Even the New Testament would approve such a silence. There are passages in the New Testament even extolling irony, so long as it is the better side that it is used to conceal. However, this movement is just as much a movement of irony as any other movement based on subjectivity's being higher than reality. This is something no one nowadays wants to know; generally people want to know no more about irony than Hegel has said about it, though curiously enough he had rather little understanding of it and indeed bore a grudge against it which our age finds good reason not to give up, seeing that for it irony is simply something it must guard itself against. The Sermon on the Mount says: 'But thou, when thou fastest, anoint thine head, and wash thy face; that thou appear not unto men to fast.' The passage gives clear testimony to subjectivity's incommensurability with reality, indeed even to its having the right to deceive. If only those people who wander about these days with vague talk of the idea of the congregation would read the New Testament, they might come upon other ideas.

But now Abraham. How did he act? For I have not forgotten, and the reader may now be pleased to recall, that this was the point to which the whole preceding discussion was intended to lead. Not to make Abraham more intelligible thereby, but in order that his unintelligibility might be seen more in the round, for, as I have said, I cannot understand Abraham, I can only admire him. It was also mentioned that none of the stages described contained an analogue of Abraham, they were elaborated only so as to indicate, from the point of view of their own sphere, the boundary of the unknown land by the points of discrepancy. If there should be any question of an analogy here it would have to be the paradox of sin, but that again belongs to another sphere and cannot explain Abraham, and is itself far easier to explain than Abraham.

So Abraham did not speak. He spoke neither to Sarah, to Eleazar, nor to Isaac. He passed over these three ethical authorities. Because for Abraham the ethical had no higher expression than that of family life.

Aesthetics allowed, in fact demanded, silence of the

individual when by remaining silent he could save another. This is already enough to show that Abraham does not lie within the circumference of aesthetics. His silence is not at all to save Isaac, as in general the whole task of sacrificing Isaac for his own and God's sake is an outrage aesthetically. Aesthetics can well understand that I sacrifice myself, but not that I should sacrifice another for my own sake. The aesthetic hero was silent. Ethics condemned him, however, because it was on the strength of his accidental particularity that he remained silent. His human prescience was what determined that he should be silent. This ethics cannot forgive. All such human insight is only an illusion. Ethics demands an infinite movement which requires disclosure. So the aesthetic hero can indeed speak but will not.

The genuine tragic hero sacrifices himself and everything he has for the universal; his action, every emotion in him belongs to the universal, he is revealed, and in this disclosure he is the beloved son of ethics. This does not apply to Abraham. He does nothing for the universal and he is concealed.

We are now at the paradox. Either the individual as the particular can stand in an absolute relation to the absolute, and then the ethical is not the highest, or Abraham is done for, he is neither a tragic hero nor an aesthetic hero.

Here again the paradox might seem the easiest and most convenient thing of all. However, I must repeat that anyone who remains convinced of that is not the knight of faith, for distress and anguish are the only justification conceivable, even though they cannot be conceived in general, for if they could the paradox would be cancelled.

Abraham is silent – but he *cannot* speak, therein lies the distress and anguish. For if when I speak I cannot make myself understood, I do not speak even if I keep talking without stop day and night. This is the case with Abraham. He can say what he will, but there is one thing he cannot say and since he cannot say it, i.e. say it in a way that another understands it, he does not speak. The relief of speech is that it translates me into the universal. Now Abraham can say the most beautiful things any language can muster about how he loves Isaac. But this is not what he has in mind, that being the deeper thought that he would have to sacrifice Isaac because it was a trial. This no one can understand, and so no one can but misunderstand the former. Of this distress the tragic hero knows nothing. In the first place he has the consolation that all counter-arguments have been done justice to, that he has been able to give Clytemnestra, Iphigenia, Achilles, the Chorus, every living being, every voice from the heart of humankind, every intelligent, every anxious, every accusing, every compassionate thought an opportunity to stand up against him. He can be sure that all that it is possible to say against him has been said, unsparingly, mercilessly – and to contend with the whole world is a comfort, but to contend with oneself dreadful. – He need have no fear of having overlooked something, of later having to cry out like King Edward IV at the news of the death of Clarence:

Who sued to me for him? Who, in my wrath,
Kneeled at my feet and bid me be advised?
Who spoke of brotherhood? Who spoke of love?

The tragic hero knows nothing of the terrible responsibility of solitude. Moreover, he has the comfort of being able to weep and wail with Clytemnestra and Iphigenia – and sobbing and crying give relief, while groans that cannot be uttered are torture. Agamemnon can rally himself quickly to the certainty that he will act, and he therefore still has time to bring comfort and courage. This Abraham cannot do. When his heart is stirred, when his words would convey a blessed consolation for the whole world, he dare not console, for would not Sarah, would not Eleazar, would not Isaac say to him, 'Why do you want to do this, you can after all refrain'? And if in his distress he should want to unburden his feelings and embrace everything dear to him before taking the final step, then this might have the most frightful consequence that Sarah, that Eleazar, that Isaac would be offended in him and believe him a hypocrite. Talk he cannot, he speaks no human language. Though he himself understood all the tongues of the world, though the loved ones understood them too – he still could not talk – he speaks a divine tongue – he 'speaks with tongues'.

This distress I can well understand. I can admire Abraham. I have no fear that anyone should be tempted by this story to want irresponsibly to be the single individual. But I also confess that I myself lack the courage for that, and that I would gladly renounce any prospect of coming further if only it were possible for me to come that far, however late in the day. Abraham can refrain at any moment, he can repent the whole thing as a temptation. Then he can speak, then all will understand him – but then he is no longer Abraham.

Abraham *cannot* speak. What would explain everything, that it is a trial – though note, one in which the ethical is the temptation – is something he cannot say (i.e. in a way that can be understood). Anyone so placed is an emigrant from the sphere of the universal. And yet what comes next he is even less able to say. For, as was made sufficiently clear earlier, Abraham makes two movements. He makes the infinite movement of resignation and gives up his claim to Isaac, something no one can understand because it is a private undertaking. But then he further makes, and at every moment is making, the movement of faith. This is his comfort. For he says, 'Nevertheless it won't happen, or if it does the Lord will give me a new Isaac on the strength of the absurd.' The tragic hero does at least get to the end of the story. Iphigenia bows to her father's decision, she herself makes the infinite movement of resignation and they now understand one another. She is able to understand Agamemnon because his undertaking expresses the universal. If on the other hand Agamemnon were to say to her, 'Even though the deity demands you as a sacrifice, it's still possible that he didn't – on the strength of the absurd', he would instantly become unintelligible to her. If he could say it on the strength of human calculation, then Iphigenia would surely understand him. But that would mean that Agamemnon had not made the infinite movement of resignation, and then he would not be a hero, and then the seer's utterance is just a traveller's tale and the whole incident a piece of vaudeville.

So Abraham did not speak. Only one word of his has been preserved, his only reply to Isaac, which we can take to be sufficient evidence that he had not spoken previously. Isaac asks Abraham where the lamb is for the burnt offering. 'And Abraham said: My son, God will provide himself a lamb for a burnt offering.'

This last word of Abraham's I shall consider here a little more closely. If it had not occurred the whole incident would lack something. If it had been a different word everything might dissolve in confusion.

I have often pondered on how far a tragic hero, whether suffering or action provides the consummation of his heroism, ought to have a final remark. So far as I can see it depends on what sphere of life he belongs to, on the extent to which his life has intellectual significance, on how far his suffering or action stand in relation to spirit.

It goes without saying that at the moment of consummation the tragic hero, like anyone else, is capable of a few words, even a few appropriate words. But the question is whether it is appropriate for him to say them. If the significance of his life consists in an outward act, then he has nothing to say, since everything he says is essentially idle chat which can only weaken the impact he makes, while the rites of tragedy require on the contrary that he fulfil his task in silence, whether in action or suffering. So as not to go too far afield I shall simply draw on our nearest example. If Agamemnon himself, and not Calchas [the seer], had had to draw the knife on Iphigenia he would only have demeaned himself by wanting to say a few words at the last moment. Everyone knew the significance of his deed, the whole process of piety, pity, feeling, and tears was done with, and besides, his life had no relation to spirit, i.e. he was not a teacher or a witness to the spirit. If on the other hand the significance of the hero's life tends towards spirit, the lack of a remark will weaken the impact he makes. It is not something appropriate he should be saying, not some bit of rhetoric, but something that will convey that he is consummating himself in the decisive moment. An intellectual tragic hero of this kind should allow himself what people often aspire to frivolously, namely having and keeping the last word. We expect of him the same exalted bearing as becomes any tragic hero, but on top of that we expect some word. So if an intellectual tragic hero consummates his heroism in suffering (in death), in this final word he will become immortal before he dies, while the ordinary tragic hero only becomes immortal after his death.

Socrates can be used as an example. He was an intellectual tragic hero. He hears his death-sentence. That instant he dies. Unless you grasp that it requires all the strength of spirit to die, that the hero always dies before his death, you will not come particularly far in your observations on life. So as a hero Socrates is required to stay calm and at ease, but as an intellectual hero he is required to have sufficient spiritual strength at the final moment to fulfil himself. So he cannot, like the ordinary tragic hero, concentrate on keeping himself face to face with death; he has to make this latter movement so quickly that in the same instant he is consciously above that conflict and continues to assert himself. Had Socrates been silent in the crisis of death he would have weakened the effect of his life, aroused a suspicion that the resilience of irony was not, in him, a primitive strength, but only a game whose flexibility he had to exploit in the decisive moment, according to an opposite standard, pathetically to sustain himself.*

What I have been briefly hinting at here doesn't really apply to Abraham, to the extent that one supposes one might find by analogy some appropriate word for Abraham; but it applies to the extent that one sees the necessity of Abraham's fulfilling himself at the final moment not by drawing the knife silently but by having something to say, seeing that as the father of faith he has absolute significance in terms of spirit. As to *what* he is to say, I can form no idea in advance. Once he has said it I can no doubt understand it, even in a sense understand Abraham *in* what is said, yet without thereby coming any nearer him than in the foregoing. If we'd had no remark from Socrates I could have put myself into his position and made one, and if I couldn't do that myself,

---

* Which of Socrates's remarks is to be regarded as the decisive one can be a matter of controversy, since Socrates has been in so many ways poetically volatilized by Plato. I suggest the following: the death-sentence is announced to him, that instant he dies and fulfils himself in the famous rejoinder that he was surprised to have been condemned with a majority of three votes. He could have found no more ironic jest in some market-place flippancy or fool's inanity than in this comment on the death-sentence which condemns him from life itself.

a poet would have managed. But no poet can reach Abraham.

Before going on to consider Abraham's last word more closely, I must first draw attention to the difficulty of Abraham's coming to say anything at all. The distress and anguish in the paradox consisted, as explained above, precisely in the silence; Abraham cannot speak.* To that extent then it is self-contradictory to demand that he should speak, unless one wants him out of the paradox again, so that in the decisive moment he suspends it, whereby he ceases to be Abraham and brings to naught all that went before. Were Abraham, at the decisive moment, to say to Isaac, 'It is you who are to be sacrificed', this would only be a weakness. For if he could speak at all he should have done so long before, and the weakness then consists in his not having the maturity of spirit and concentration to imagine the whole of the pain beforehand but having pushed some of it aside so that the actual pain proves greater than the imagined one. Besides, with talk of this kind he would fall out of the paradox, and if he really wanted to talk to Isaac he would have to transform his own situation into that of a temptation. Otherwise, after all, he could say nothing and if he does so transform his situation he isn't even a tragic hero.

---

* In so far as there is any question of an analogy [here], the circumstances of the death of Pythagoras provide one. In his last moments Pythagoras had to consummate the silence he had always maintained, and so he *said*, 'It's better to be killed than to speak.' cf. Diogenes, 8th Bk. § 39.

Nevertheless a last word of Abraham's *has* been preserved, and so far as I can understand the paradox I can
also understand Abraham's total presence in that word.
First and foremost he doesn't say anything, and that is
his way of saying what he has to say. His answer to Isaac
has the form of irony, for it is always irony to say
something and yet not say it. Isaac asks Abraham because
he assumes Abraham knows. Now if Abraham had
replied, 'I know nothing', he would have uttered an
untruth. He cannot say anything, since what he knows
he cannot say. So he replies, 'My son, God will provide
himself a lamb for a burnt offering.' Here one sees the
double movement in Abraham's soul, as it has been
described in the foregoing. Had Abraham simply
renounced his claim to Isaac and done no more, he
would have uttered an untruth. He knows that God
demands the sacrifice of Isaac, and he knows that precisely at this moment he himself is ready to sacrifice him.
So, after having made this movement Abraham has at
every instant been performing the next, making the
movement on the strength of the absurd. To that extent
he utters no untruth, for on the strength of the absurd it
is after all possible that God might do something quite
different. He utters no untruth then, but neither does he
say anything, for he speaks in a foreign tongue. This
becomes still more obvious when we consider that it
was Abraham himself who was to sacrifice Isaac. If the
task had been a different one, if the Lord had commanded
Abraham to take Isaac out on the mountain in Moriah,
and then let his own lightning strike Isaac and take
him as a sacrifice in that way, Abraham would in a

straightforward sense be right to talk as enigmatically as he did, for in that case he himself could not have known what would happen. But as the task is given to Abraham, it is he who must act, so he must know at the decisive moment what he is about to do, and accordingly must know that Isaac is to be sacrificed. If he doesn't definitely know that, he hasn't made the infinite movement of resignation, in which case his words are not indeed untrue, but then at the same time he is very far from being Abraham, he is less significant than a tragic hero, he is in fact an irresolute man who can resolve to do neither one thing nor the other, and who will therefore always come to talk in riddles. But such a *Haesitator* [waverer] is simply a parody of the knight of faith.

Here too it can appear that one can understand Abraham, but only as one understands the paradox. For my part I can in a way understand Abraham, but I see very well that I lack the courage to speak in this way, as much as I lack the courage to act like Abraham. But I do not at all say that what he did is inconsiderable on that account, since on the contrary it is the one and only marvel.

And what did contemporaries think of the tragic hero? That he was great, and they looked up to him. And that noble assembly of worthies, the jury that every generation appoints to pass judgement on its predecessor, came to the same verdict. But none could understand Abraham. And yet think what he achieved! To remain true to his love. But he who loves God has no need of tears, needs no admiration, and forgets his suffering in love, indeed forgets so completely that afterwards not the least hint of his pain would remain were God himself not to remember it; for God sees in secret and knows the distress and counts the tears and forgets nothing.

So either there is a paradox, that the single individual as the particular stands in an absolute relation to the absolute, or Abraham is done for.

Epilogue

Once when the spice market in Holland was a little slack, the merchants had some cargoes dumped at sea to force up the price. That was a pardonable, perhaps necessary, stratagem. Is it something similar we need in the world of spirit? Are we so convinced of having reached the heights that there is nothing left but piously to believe we still haven't come that far, so as at least to have something to fill the time with? Is it this kind of trick of self-deception the present generation needs, is it to a virtuosity in this it should be educated, or has it not already perfected itself sufficiently in the art of self-deception? Or is what it needs not rather an honest seriousness which fearlessly and incorruptibly calls attention to the tasks, an honest seriousness that lovingly fences the tasks about, which does not frighten people into wanting to dash precipitately to the heights, but keeps the tasks young and beautiful and charming to behold, and inviting to all, yet hard too and an inspiration to noble minds, since noble natures are only inspired by difficulty? However much one generation learns from another, it can never learn from its predecessor the genuinely human factor. In this respect every generation begins afresh, has no task other than that of any previous generation, and comes no further, provided the latter hasn't shirked its task and deceived itself. This authenti-

cally human factor is passion, in which the one generation also fully understands the other and understands
itself. Thus no generation has learned from another
how to love, no generation can begin other than at the
beginning, the task of no later generation is shorter than
its predecessor's, and if someone, unlike the previous
generation, is unwilling to stay with love but wants to
go further, then that is simply idle and foolish talk.

But the highest passion in a human being is faith,
and here no generation begins other than where its
predecessor did, every generation begins from the beginning, the succeeding generation comes no further than
the previous one, provided the latter was true to its task
and didn't betray it. That this sounds wearying is not of
course for the generation to say, for it is indeed the
generation that has the task and it has nothing to do
with the fact that the previous generation had the same
task, unless that particular generation or the individuals
in it presumed to occupy the position to which only
the spirit that governs the world, and which has the
endurance not to grow weary, is entitled. If that is the
kind of thing the generation begins to do, it is perverted,
and what wonder then if the whole of existence should
look perverted to it? For surely no one has found life
more perverted than the tailor in the fairy-tale who got
to heaven in his lifetime and from there looked down
on the world. So long as the generation only worries
about its task, which is the highest it can attain to, it
cannot grow weary. That task is always enough for a
human lifetime. When children on holiday get through
all their games by noon and then ask impatiently, 'Can't

anyone think of a new game?', does this show that they are more developed and advanced than children of the same or a previous generation who could make the games they already know last the whole day? Or does it not rather show that those children lack what I would call the good-natured seriousness that belongs to play?

Faith is the highest passion in a human being. Many in every generation may not come that far, but none comes further. Whether there are also many who do not discover it in our own age I leave open. I can only refer to my own experience, that of one who makes no secret of the fact that he has far to go, yet without therefore wishing to deceive either himself or what is great by reducing this latter to a triviality, to a children's disease which one must hope to get over as soon as possible. But life has tasks enough, even for one who fails to come as far as faith, and when he loves these honestly life won't be a waste either, even if it can never compare with that of those who had a sense of the highest and grasped it. But anyone who comes to faith (whether he be greatly talented or simple-minded makes no difference) won't remain at a standstill there. Indeed he would be shocked if anyone said this to him. Just as the lover would be indignant if someone said he had come to a standstill in his love, for he would reply, 'I'm by no means standing still in my love, for I have my life in it.' And yet he too doesn't come any further, not to anything else. For when he finds that out he has another explanation.

'One must go further, one must go further.' This need to go on is of ancient standing. Heraclitus the 'obscure' who reposited his thoughts in his writings and his writings in the Temple of Diana (for his thoughts had been his armour in life, which he therefore hung up in the temple of the goddess), the obscure Heraclitus has said, 'One can never walk through the same river twice.'* The obscure Heraclitus had a disciple who didn't remain standing there but went further and added, 'One cannot do it even once.'† Poor Heraclitus to have such a disciple! This improvement changed the Heraclitian principle into an Eleatic doctrine denying movement, and yet all that disciple wanted was to be a disciple of Heraclitus who went further, not back to what Heraclitus had abandoned.

---

* 'Chai potamou roi apeikadzon ta onta legei hos dis es ton auton potamon ouk embaiis.' cf. Plato's *Cratyllus* §402, Ast. 3rd B. Pag. 158.
† cf. Tennemann *Gesch. d. Philos.* Ister B. Pag. 220.

FOR THE BEST IN PAPERBACKS, LOOK FOR THE

In every corner of the world, on every subject under the sun, Penguin represents quality and variety—the very best in publishing today.

For complete information about books available from Penguin—including Penguin Classics, Penguin Compass, and Puffins—and how to order them, write to us at the appropriate address below. Please note that for copyright reasons the selection of books varies from country to country.

In the United States: Please write to *Penguin Group (USA), P.O. Box 12289 Dept. B, Newark, New Jersey 07101-5289* or call 1-800-788-6262.

In the United Kingdom: Please write to *Dept. EP, Penguin Books Ltd, Bath Road, Harmondsworth, West Drayton, Middlesex UB7 0DA.*

In Canada: Please write to *Penguin Books Canada Ltd, 90 Eglinton Avenue East, Suite 700, Toronto, Ontario M4P 2Y3.*

In Australia: Please write to *Penguin Books Australia Ltd, P.O. Box 257, Ringwood, Victoria 3134.*

In New Zealand: Please write to *Penguin Books (NZ) Ltd, Private Bag 102902, North Shore Mail Centre, Auckland 10.*

In India: Please write to *Penguin Books India Pvt Ltd, 11 Panchsheel Shopping Centre, Panchsheel Park, New Delhi 110 017.*

In the Netherlands: Please write to *Penguin Books Netherlands bv, Postbus 3507, NL-1001 AH Amsterdam.*

In Germany: Please write to *Penguin Books Deutschland GmbH, Metzlerstrasse 26, 60594 Frankfurt am Main.*

In Spain: Please write to *Penguin Books S. A., Bravo Murillo 19, 1° B, 28015 Madrid.*

In Italy: Please write to *Penguin Italia s.r.l., Via Benedetto Croce 2, 20094 Corsico, Milano.*

In France: Please write to *Penguin France, Le Carré Wilson, 62 rue Benjamin Baillaud, 31500 Toulouse.*

In Japan: Please write to *Penguin Books Japan Ltd, Kaneko Building, 2-3-25 Koraku, Bunkyo-Ku, Tokyo 112.*

In South Africa: Please write to *Penguin Books South Africa (Pty) Ltd, Private Bag X14, Parkview, 2122 Johannesburg.*